The Complete Book of Flying

The Complete Book of FLYING

produced by Lyle Kenyon Engel

text by Monty Norris

FOUR WINDS PRESS   NEW YORK

Library of Congress Cataloging in Publication Data

Engel, Lyle Kenyon.
The complete book of flying.

Includes index.
SUMMARY: Discusses the basic principles of aeronautics and
instructions received at a typical flight school.
1. Airplanes—Piloting. [1. Flight training] I. Norris,
Monty. II. Title.
TL710.E6   629.132′5   76–17865
ISBN 0-590-17377-4

Published by Four Winds Press
A Division of Scholastic Magazines, Inc., New York, N.Y.
Printed in the United States of America
Library of Congress Catalog Card Number: 76–17865
1   2   3   4   5   80   79   78   77   76

Contents

Introduction

How many times have you thought, "Gee, it'd be a great idea to go skiing this weekend, but with that long drive facing us, I don't know if it's worth the trouble." Or, "Boy, wouldn't it be fun to head south for the weekend? It'd be great to come back Monday with a tan in the middle of all this snow. But it takes so long to get there."

Learning to fly is the answer. And it's never been more available.

Maybe you've discovered recently that a friend is a pilot, and that's caused you to think: "He doesn't seem *unusual*. His family doesn't have any more money than mine. He isn't any more mechanically minded than I am. I never thought of him as some kind of *daredevil*.

And he certainly isn't any *smarter* than I am!"

Or maybe you're just a little hesitant about trying something new. I remember a few years ago when a woman colleague of mine in her fifties started taking flying lessons. I was both a little startled and envious. If *she* could learn to fly an airplane, what in the world was stopping *me?*

Nothing really.

If your picture of flying has been formed from watching movies or reading newspapers, you may be forgiven if you think pilots are flamboyant and a little kooky and that a large number of "small" airplanes crash. It's true that some private airplanes crash each year—but the figure, according to the Federal Aviation Administration (FAA), represents about *one twenty-fifth of one percent* of the total fleet. Pilots are no less human than skiers, sailors or motorists. Accidents happen in any kind of activity.

You might think, too, that the more than 40,000 women pilots flying small airplanes today are unusual. But most of these "airmen," as the FAA illogically insists on calling them, are mostly housewives, secretaries, teachers and mothers. Almost a thousand are qualified flight instructors, and this scribe was somewhat surprised, when I finally quit making excuses and decided to take the big step, that my instructor would be a woman—attractive, middle-aged and the mother of four.

Icarus may have started it all back in the days of Greek mythology when he escaped from Crete with artificial wings. But that first recorded flight—in legend at least—didn't go very well. The heat melted the wax that fastened his wings, and Icarus plunged into the Aegean Sea. There were hundreds, perhaps even thousands, of attempts by man to fly in the ensuing centuries, but air transportation remains a purely twentieth-century phenomenon. It has developed with almost incredible swiftness from scarcely noted experiments on the hills of Kitty Hawk, North Carolina, in 1903, to its role today as a major industry and vital public necessity which touches the lives of everyone. General aviation employs some 120,000 persons in manufacturing, servicing and flying, and by the end of this decade, its economic impact, both direct and indirect, may reach $18 *billion* a year.

The term *general aviation* refers to all civilian aviation activity except commercial airlines. Statistically, about 70 percent of all general aviation flying—some 20 million hours per year—is for business or commercial purposes. General aviation carries one in three intercity air passengers—about 70 million passengers a year—and 60 percent of those passengers fly from airports that are not served by the airlines.

Because flying offers fast, safe and relatively inexpensive travel, airplanes have become increasingly important business tools in recent years as American industry has decentralized and moved away from the major metropolitan areas. Today, thousands of firms own a total of some 40,000 aircraft to carry on their business more efficiently and profitably, and many more thousands of businesses regularly charter or rent airplanes.

A recent survey showed that 432 companies of the 1000 biggest, as listed by *Fortune* magazine, operated general aviation aircraft. And the survey also revealed that those 432 companies accounted for 77 percent of the total group's sales and 84 percent of net profit.

But there are also many public benefits derived from general aviation. The U.S. balance of payments benefits, too. Since 1965, the American general aviation industry has exported nearly $1 billion worth of aircraft, and today one of every four general aviation planes produced in this country is shipped abroad. As a result, 85 percent of the total world fleet of airplanes is American-made.

Air pollution, another major concern of communities both large and small, is virtually nonexistent with general aviation. More than 90 percent of all flying is above 3000 feet, where emissions are negligible and don't effect the breathable atmosphere. Sulfur oxides, considered the most harmful pollutants, are refined out of aviation fuels, and aircraft engines are far more efficient, cleaner and better maintained than other types of engines.

In recent years, there has been much discussion about "crowded skies" and airport congestion in the United States. There are about 140,000 general aviation airplanes and some 3000 airliners in this country today. And if every one of these aircraft were in the air at the same time and at the same altitude over the state of Montana, there would still be more than a mile between their wing tips!

But this big picture of flying may mean little to you.

Maybe you're someone who wants a quicker way of getting away on the weekend or at vacation time, or you simply think learning to fly would be fun. Newspapers frequently carry stories about the annual Powder Puff Derby or accounts of someone trying to fly nonstop from Casablanca to Las Vegas, but they seldom note the thousands of citizens who use their airplanes every weekend for much less sensational outings. If you've ever tried to take a vacation with a family of six by airline, bus or car, you don't have to be told that, financially and emotionally, there has to be a better way!

Some of us think we've found it.

And one other point: The next time you meet someone who has a private pilot's license, don't bother to say, "Gee, I've always wanted to learn to fly, but. . . ." We know all the excuses by heart. And we don't believe them. But the real question is: *Do you?*

Monty Norris
Sebastopol, California

1
Why
and
How
Airplanes
Fly

It isn't magic—although flying always seems somehow kind of magical: man-made machines, soaring across the sky, turning lazily and gracefully, droning motors the only clue to their mechanical nature.

But what keeps them up there? The most common explanation for why an airplane flies is usually that it "floats" on air. And that's not bad. We're going to look at it in a little more detail, but if you keep that basic concept in mind, you'll be off to a good start. You don't have to be a scientific wizard to understand how an airplane flies. Nor do you have to be a daredevil or mechanical genius to learn how to fly. If this were necessary, then the number of pilots in the world would be reduced to about two percent of the present figure, with the author among those in the larger group.

Air usually appears to us as a weightless, invisible entity. We seldom think of it as having the ability to exert any kind of force—much less sustain an airplane in flight. Yet, we need only think of wind—or, going to the extreme, hurricanes and tornadoes—to realize that air may indeed exert considerable force.

A pilot must use, or capitalize on, the force of air in much the same way (although with greater freedom of movement and direction) that a skipper works with currents and swells when guiding a boat. And like the skipper, pilots must learn about and be constantly aware of weather and turbulence. From the first day you climb into an airplane as a student pilot these elements become an integral part of your world. For the boat skipper, turbulence comes in the form of choppy water, swells, waves and currents, while the airplane pilot must cope with crosswinds and turbulence—meaning irregular air currents such as up- and downdrafts. Only in severe cases, however, will wind actually present a special problem. But learning to cope with these situations is an important part of pilot training, even at the beginning level. During takeoffs and landings, simple turns and even straight and level flight, pilots must learn to work with wind currents and turbulence.

But before we get too involved in flying maneuvers (which will be covered extensively later in the book) let's stay with aerodynamics for a while and find out why an airplane flies—assuming, of course, the pilot is doing everything correctly.

AERODYNAMICS

Most of us realize an airplane could not fly without wings any more than a bird could. But wings are more than just appendages sticking out the side of the airplane's fuselage or body shell. These wings, as they are usually called, are actually *airfoils* specially designed for their job. To understand how and why, we'll explore some simple physics.

The most significant physical law governing design of the airfoil is the *Bernoulli principle*, which states the relationship between pressure, fluid-flow velocity and the potential energy of fluids (liquids and gases, including air). This principle, discovered by Daniel Bernoulli (1700–1782), a Swiss scientist, states that "as the velocity of the fluid increases, the pressure in the fluid decreases." Conversely, "as the velocity of the fluid decreases, the pressure in the fluid increases."

As an example, let's look at the *venturi tube,* which is narrower in the middle than it is at either end. As air passes through the tube, it speeds up as it reaches the narrow portion and slows down again as it passes the restriction. The reason is that, assuming the air flowing through the tube has 1000 molecules per inch and is moving at one inch per second, there are 1000 molecules flowing through the tube each second. If the narrow part is one half the size of the large ends, the molecules must speed up to maintain equilibrium, or

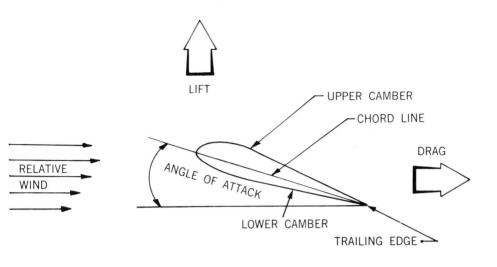

The aerodynamics of a wing.

in other words, to keep moving 1000 molecules through the tube at the same rate—which is 1000 per second. More energy is imparted to the molecules as they accelerate, which leaves less energy to exert pressure, and the pressure thus decreases. The throat of a carburetor is an example of the venturi principle.

The same principle is involved in creating lift for an airplane. Actually, most of the airplane, including the nose, fuselage and tail assembly, is designed with aerodynamics in mind, but the wings are the main part of an airplane that support the machine when it's airborne. An airfoil has a leading edge, a trailing edge, a chord and camber.

The *leading edge* is that part of the airfoil which meets the oncoming air. In other words, the front. The *trailing edge* is the aft or rear end of the airfoil where the airflow over the upper surface joins the airflow over the lower surface (unless you happen to be flying backward, in which case aerodynamics won't help you at all). The *chord line* is an imaginary straight line drawn from the leading edge to the trailing edge. This line has significance only in determining the *angle of attack* of an airfoil and in determining wing area. Angle of attack, probably one of the most misunderstood terms in aviation for the beginner or outsider, simply means the angle at which the airfoil or wing is meeting the oncoming air. (It has absolutely nothing to do with aerial combat.) *Camber* of an airfoil is the curvature of its upper (upper camber) and lower (lower camber) surfaces.

THE FOUR FORCES

Lift would seem to be the singularly most important force acting on an airplane in flight, but there are actually three other forces of equal importance to the pilot. *Lift* is the upward acting force; *gravity*, or weight, is the downward force; *thrust* moves the airplane forward; and *drag* resists thrust and slows the airplane down.

Lift. The wings' job is to achieve as much lift as necessary to hold the airplane up in the air. The distance that the air must travel over the curved top of the wing is greater than the distance it must move along the bottom. As the air moves over the top, it speeds up in an attempt to reestablish equilibrium at the rear of the airfoil. Because of this extra speed, the air exerts less sideways pressure on the top surface of the wing than on the bottom, and lift is produced. The pressure on the bottom of the wing is normally increased also, and on an average, this contributes about 25 percent of the lift. This percentage, however, varies with angle of attack. Newton's law—"For every action there is an equal and opposite reaction"—also applies here. The wing deflects the airflow downward with a reaction of the airplane being sustained in flight—or floating on air, as some people think of it. Some engineers prefer using Newton's law to Bernoulli's, but the latter offers a clearer picture of why there are opposing forces operating to keep an airplane aloft.

Lift opposes weight, and thrust opposes drag. When an airplane is in straight and level flight, the opposing forces balance each other—meaning lift equals weight (gravity) and thrust equals drag. Let's return to that term we used a while back—*angle of attack*. An airplane's wings get an additional boost because of the angle at which they are inclined. As the airplane moves forward, the air hitting the underside of the wing actually gives it additional lift. You can test this theory by holding your hand out the window of a car while riding along at highway speeds. As you tilt your hand up slightly you'll notice the wind tends to push it up. That may not be the most scientific method of proving a principle, but it works. During slow flight, which is an important part of a student pilot's training, engine power (thrust) is reduced and the angle of attack increased.

Increasing the angle of attack will increase lift up to a point. As the airfoil is inclined, the air moving over the top is diverted over a greater distance. But

SWEPT-BACK WING

RECTANGULAR WING

DELTA WING

ELLIPTICAL WING

TAPERED
LEADING-EDGE WING

TAPERED
TRAILING-EDGE WING

DOUBLE-TAPERED WING

Top view of various wing configurations.

as the angle of attack continues to increase, it becomes difficult for the air to flow smoothly across the top of the wing. At a certain point, depending on design of the wing and relative thrust, the air starts breaking up into a burbling or turbulent pattern. This turbulence results in a loss of lift, and a *stall* results.

A stall when flying is not at all the same thing as when your car stalls. An airplane may stall when the engine is running perfectly. What happens is that the wing is no longer doing its job by providing the airplane with enough lift to keep it airborne. The angle of attack at which most airplanes will stall is about 20 degrees, but that can vary considerably depending both on how much power the airplane has and is using at the time and on wing design. Some aerobatic and fighter aircraft can actually be flown almost straight up for a distance before they will stall out. This is primarily a combination of thrust (horsepower) and lift (wing design). *Every* airplane, however, has a point at which it will eventually stall if the pilot doesn't take some corrective measures. It is important during flight training for pilots to learn how to stall an airplane and then recover. We'll talk more about that experience in Chapter 5.

As you might already suspect, the shape and size of a wing in proportion to the fuselage are important to the performance of an airplane. Wing design is usually determined on the basis of what the airplane is to be used for. If an airplane is designed for slow speeds, it will have a thicker wing than an airplane used for high speed.

Planform is the word used to describe the shape of

wings as seen from directly above or below. The relationship between the length and width of a wing is called the *aspect ratio*. This is computed by dividing the span (distance from wing tip to wing tip) by the average chord of the wing. Generally, the higher the aspect ratio the more efficient the wing. A long, narrow wing will create more lift per square foot of area than a short, wide wing. The aspect ratios on gliders can be as much as 30 to 1, while the average aspect ratio of most small airplanes is about 6 to 1.

Gravity. Like the common cold and taxes, gravity is something the pilot has to learn to live with. It's the force that lift has to overcome if the airplane is going to fly. But unlike a bird, an airplane doesn't flap its wings (or shouldn't) in order to generate thrust.

Thrust. Forward motion is necessary to get a fixed-wing aircraft off the ground and keep it there. This is where the engine and propeller (or jet engine) enter the picture. It's another example of Newton's law. The propeller takes a large mass of air and accelerates it rearward, resulting in the equal and opposite reaction of the plane moving forward. The airplane engine develops horsepower within its cylinders and, by rotating a propeller, exerts thrust. The propeller, like the wings, is actually a sophisticated airfoil designed to carve its way smoothly through the air with a minimum of resistance or drag.

Drag. Any time a body is moved through liquid or gas (including air) it encounters resistance, called *drag*.

An airplane is designed to reduce drag as much as possible, which improves both performance and economy. But even the sleekest jet fighter with its bullet nose and delta wings meets some resistance as it sizzles through the air at several times the speed of sound. "Total" drag on an airplane is composed of two main types—parasite drag and induced drag.

Parasite drag is present any time the airplane is moving. It comes from friction between the airplane itself and the atmosphere, and it can never be totally eliminated, regardless of design. Parasite drag is also referred to as "form" drag because it is based entirely on the components of the airplane, such as the wings, fuselage, tail assembly and landing gear. Even the spinning propeller and a tiny radio antenna contribute to this kind of drag. As the name implies, parasite drag is a drain on performance and about as welcome as any other parasite. Through streamlining of the airplane and using such features as retractable landing gear, designers can reduce parasite drag considerably —but never entirely.

Induced drag results from lift. Ironically, the turbulence in the air created by the airplane as it moves along is what produces this form of drag. Increasing the angle of attack, decreasing speed or applying flaps (which will be explained shortly) all increase induced drag.

AIRPLANE ANATOMY

Wings. Most airplanes today, as even a casual walk around an airport will show, are *monoplanes,* or airplanes with one wing on each side. This can be a confusing term for some of us, however, because we generally think of airplanes as having two wings— one on each side of the fuselage or body. The term *monoplane* evolved in an era when many airplanes had double wings—one on top of the other—and were called *biplanes*. Perhaps, in hindsight, it would have been better to have called these aircraft something else—like *triplanes* or *quadraplanes*. But we didn't. So now we're stuck with a rather awkward bit of nomenclature. Don't let this bother you. Just accept the terminology. Most biplanes today are likely to be used for agricultural purposes, such as crop dusting, or they are restored antiques or sport airplanes made from a kit or designed and built at home.

Even among the monoplanes, however, there seems to be an infinite variety of wing shapes and locations in relationship to the fuselage (see illustration). Almost all small airplanes today are either high- or low-wing monoplanes. Some use wing braces, while others support the wings internally. The differences between high- and low-winged aircraft are more a matter of personal taste than they are a question of performance or reliability. Low-winged airplanes, however, have a lower center of gravity and wider-track landing gear, which does improve landing stability.

Wings are designed to be extremely strong and, at the same time, lightweight. *Spars* run the length of the wing, from wing root to wing tip, and bear the major portion of bending loads. Bending or twisting loads are transferred to the metal skin and absorbed

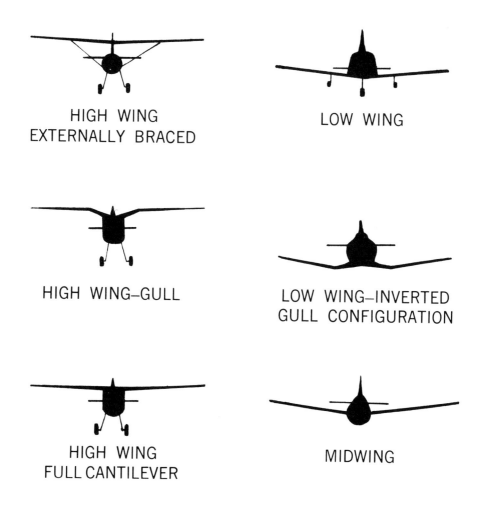

HIGH WING
EXTERNALLY BRACED

LOW WING

HIGH WING–GULL

LOW WING–INVERTED
GULL CONFIGURATION

HIGH WING
FULL CANTILEVER

MIDWING

Frontal view of various wing configurations.

by tension or compression of the skin. *Ribs* maintain the shape of the wing, stiffen the skin and transmit loads to the spars. Additional resistance to skin buckling is provided by *stringers* and *formers*. In almost all airplanes, fuel tanks are mounted inside each wing. *Flaps* and *ailerons* are hinged along the trailing edge of the wings. Ailerons are located on the outside trailing edge of the wing and move in opposite directions (up and down) to make the airplane roll or bank. Flaps are mounted on the inside trailing edge of the wing and move together in only one direction—down. Flaps are used almost exclusively during takeoffs and landings.

Fuselage. The fuselage is the body of the airplane and provides an enclosed cabin or cockpit for the pilot and passengers, a place for baggage and housing for the controls and instruments. Most modern light planes and training aircraft utilize a durable semimonocoque type of construction, which means that the skin, made of stamped and formed sheets of aluminum alloy, carries a major share of the stresses. The rest of the structural strength comes from internal members called *bulkheads, stiffeners* and *stringers.*

Monocoque construction is a major improvement over the old cloth-covered frame fuselages of the past, because it is safer, stronger, more weather resistant and soundproof. The cabin in modern airplanes (the term *cockpit* has all but disappeared from aviation jargon) is usually as plush (and sometimes gaudy) as the interior of an automobile, complete with pile carpet, imitation wood paneling, armrests, heater and even air conditioning as optional equipment. Insulation and aerodynamics are so improved today that even in light trainers like the Piper Cherokee you can carry on a conversation in *almost* normal tones even during a full-throttle climb.

Empennage. *Empennage* is a term describing the tail assembly, which in most airplanes includes a fixed vertical stabilizer, attached movable rudder, horizontal stabilizer and hinged movable elevator. There are several variations on this, however, such as the butterfly or V-shaped tail assembly of the Beechcraft Bonanza. And in recent years, technology has given us still another advance on an old theme in the form of the *stabilator*, which is a pivoting one-piece horizontal stabilizer.

Landing Gear. Although an airplane is designed and built expressly for flying, it still spends the majority of its life on the ground. Provisions must be made for it to maneuver around on the ground and get rolling fast enough to take off, as well as to land smoothly and safely. This is where the landing gear comes in.

The landing gear of an airplane may be the *tail-wheel* type (the term you'll hear most around airports is "tail dragger"), which incorporates two main wheels and a steerable tail wheel, or it may be the newer *tricycle* variety, with two main wheels and a steerable nosewheel. The landing gear may be fixed in position or, through a hydraulic retracting system, drawn up into the wings or fuselage, which greatly improves aerodynamics and reduces drag.

Not all airplanes, however, are designed to land on solid ground. Some are fitted with giant skis for landings on the ice and snow, while still others use pontoons for landing on water. Pilots utilizing ski-equipped airplanes can operate from frozen lakes, glaciers and snowbound airports. Floats and amphibious gears permit pilots to land at vacation resorts and remote locations where lakes and rivers are the only landing areas.

Power Plant. The most frequently used power plant in modern light airplanes is the gasoline-powered internal-combustion engine. In single-engine aircraft, an engine mounting holds the power plant to a sealed fire wall at the front of the cabin section. A cowling is used to enclose the engine and also provide cooling by ducting air around the engine cylinders as well as streamlining the front of the airplane to reduce drag and wind noise. The cowling also protects the engine and its components from the weather—and it makes the airplane look a lot better.

Propellers. In a sense, the propeller is a revolving wing. It's mounted directly on the engine crankshaft, which is driven by the engine pistons, and spins as the engine goes through its power cycle. Each blade of the propeller is shaped like a small airfoil or wing. Blades are "twisted" to ensure that the propeller bites into the air at the correct angle and provides forward lift or thrust. The propeller rotates clockwise, causing a rotating mass of air to be pushed toward the tail of the airplane with the opposite reaction of the airplane moving forward through the air.

FLIGHT CONTROLS

Most light airplanes have four basic controls which are used to operate them both on the ground and in

The instrument panel and controls in the 150-horsepower Piper Cherokee. Notice the toe brakes on the rudder pedals—a convenient feature introduced recently. The hand brake is located under the tachometer. The hand lever just below the microphone cord operates the flaps.

the air. Controls on modern airplanes are divided into primary and secondary systems. Primary controls are those which are necessary for safe flight, such as throttle, ailerons, elevator (or stabilator) and rudder. Secondary controls improve the performance of the airplane and relieve the pilot of some work. These secondary controls are the flaps and trim-tab system.

Throttle. The throttle controls the engine power, giving the airplane the necessary thrust to fly and remain airborne, change speeds during cruise, climb or lose altitude.

Rudder. Just as the rudder of a boat or ship projects downward in the water and is used for steering, the rudder of an airplane sticks up in the air on the tail assembly and is used for guiding the direction of the airplane. The rudder is mounted on the trailing edge of the vertical stabilizer and swings to the right or left. Movement of the rudder is controlled by rudder pedals, which are connected to the rudder through a series of cables, pulleys and bell cranks. These pedals are located under the instrument panel near the floor of the pilot's compartment.

Rudder in full right-turn position.

Push the left rudder pedal and the airplane's nose moves to the left. Push the right pedal and the opposite occurs. What happens when the right rudder pedal is depressed, for example, is that the rudder swings to the right, creating a low-pressure area on the left side and a high-pressure area on the right side. This causes the tail of the airplane to move left and the nose to move to the right.

Unlike your automobile, however, which you steer with a wheel held in your hands, an airplane is steered on the ground with your feet by pushing the rudder pedals. This usually creates a little confusion for most student pilots, but it doesn't take more than a couple of hours in the airplane before most of us adjust.

On airplanes with a tail wheel, the rudder is connected to the tail wheel by coil springs, and the tail wheel serves to guide the airplane on the ground. In new aircraft with what is called tricycle landing gear, mechanical linkage connects the rudder pedals with the nosewheel for ground control.

The word *rudder* is a misleading term in aviation, however, because while the rudder of a boat is the main device for steering, the rudder on an airplane can perform its job only in conjunction with the ailerons.

Ailerons. Ailerons are used to bank the airplane—which must bank in order to turn, although banking alone will not turn the airplane. A coordinated effort using both the rudder and the ailerons is necessary for a smooth turn. Ailerons are operated with a control wheel similar to the steering wheel in an automobile.

Top: Ailerons in left-bank position.
Bottom: Ailerons in right-bank position.

This control wheel has replaced the stick used in the days of biplanes, Piper Cubs and prop-driven fighter planes.

The ailerons are located on the outside trailing edge of each wing. When the control wheel is rotated to the left, the right aileron moves down and the left aileron moves up. The downward deflected right aileron provides the right wing with increased camber on the upper surface. This creates a higher velocity airflow over the wing and a low-pressure area on the upper surface which forces the right wing upward. Conversely, the left aileron, being deflected up, forces the left wing down by decreasing the lift produced by the left outer wing panel. When the control wheel is turned to the right, an opposite aileron movement takes place, and the airplane rolls to the right.

You can't turn the airplane by banking alone, however. It is possible to turn the airplane with the rudder only, but this is a clumsy—and often dangerous—skidding maneuver accomplished by forcing one wing to move faster than the other and takes several times longer than by using both rudder and ailerons in a smooth, coordinated effort.

Elevators or Stabilator. The horizontal section of the tail assembly—which may be either the more traditional elevator style or the modern and efficient stabilator variety—governs the up-and-down direction of the airplane. Moving the elevators or stabilator up or down pitches the nose of the airplane, which changes the angle of attack of the wings. The traditional elevator system used a fixed horizontal stabilizer with flaps on the trailing edge that moved up and down in unison. The stabilator is a one-piece, horizontal tail surface that pivots up and down. Aerodynamically, the stabilator is more efficient than elevators because all of the horizontal surface moves in the stabilator design, while only a part of the surface moves with the stabilizer-elevator combination. Because of their greater efficiency, stabilators are smaller than stabilizer-elevator combinations and therefore offer much less parasite drag.

To operate the stabilator the pilot pulls back or

Above: The stabilator in the level position. Below left: Stabilator in full up position, which pushes the tail down and the nose up. Below right: The stabilator in full down position, which lifts the tail up and forces the nose down.

pushes forward on the control wheel. Pulling back on the controls moves the stabilator (or the elevators) in an up position, thereby forcing the tail down and the nose of the airplane up. The opposite is used, along with a reduction in engine power, to lose altitude. It is important to remember, however, that the pilot must always coordinate climbs and descents with an appropriate increase or reduction in thrust or power. Without added power, pulling back on the controls (raising the stabilator) will only reduce airspeed and lead to an eventual stall. A nose-down attitude without the corresponding reduction in power will allow the airplane to descend but also cause it to build up excessive speed in what is popularly called a "power dive." Such maneuvers can cause stress damage to the airplane, as well as overrev the engine.

Trim Tab. Although secondary controls are not used as frequently as the primary system, they are no less important to the pilot. With the trim tab a pilot adjusts the elevators or stabilator to maintain level flight once he has reached cruising altitude. Although in most light airplanes the pilot must still operate the controls, using the trim adjustment makes the job a lot less tedious and tiring since the airplane is adjusted to the best angle of attack for level flight. Only minor corrections and changes of direction will then usually be necessary. Without the trim equipment you would be constantly pulling back on the controls to keep the plane in level flight. Even in a small trainer and on short flights this would be very tiring and tedious.

27

Above: Flaps in the normal or full up position.
Below: One notch of flaps.

Above: Two notches of flaps.
Below: Full flaps.

On the Piper Cherokee the trim tab is a wheel located beside the pilot's seat. A tab-position indicator is incorporated in the tab-control mechanism to show the nose-up or nose-down position of the tab setting. When you first learn to fly, the trim tab seems like some kind of nuisance. But after a few hours in the air you quickly recognize it as an invaluable assistant!

Flaps. Mounted on the inside trailing edge of the wing, flaps are used almost exclusively during landings—although they can help increase lift considerably for short-field takeoffs.

Because of their added drag, however, most pilots using them for takeoffs will wait until the airplane has reached takeoff speed before dropping them. Once the flaps are then dropped, the airplane seems to literally jump into the air.

Flaps are most frequently used for landings, however. The increased lift, along with the added drag, allows you to descend more steeply without gaining unwanted airspeed. Flaps should never be used at cruising speeds since dropping them could cause severe structural damage. In fact, most airplane manufacturers forbid use of flaps during cruising speeds and specify a maximum speed at which flaps should be dropped. How much flap can be dropped varies from airplane to airplane. Some have two notches available, while others, like the Piper Cherokee, have three. On the Cherokee the flaps can be dropped to angles of 10, 25 and 40 degrees, and are operated manually by a lever on the floor which resembles the parking brake on a sports car. Flaps on other aircraft may be operated manually, hydraulically or electrically.

FLIGHT INSTRUMENTS

Most drivers, it seems, generally hop blissfully into their cars, stuff the key into the ignition, start the engine and drive away—rarely even glancing at the instruments before them. And, except on those embarrassing occasions when someone runs out of gas or the engine heats up because there wasn't any water in the radiator, we rarely suffer for such negligence. A few— and they are very few—pilots live the same way. Miraculously, most of them, too, survive.

If there is anything during your flight training that any instructor worth his or her wings and salary will try to impress upon you, it will be *instrument awareness*. You'll probably feel a little intimidated when you first climb into the cabin and look at the maze of dials facing you. Or you may wonder if you'll remember where a certain instrument is when you need it. Relax. You've just developed lazy habits as a motorist. Within the first couple of hours of flight training you'll be able to scan the instrument panel and make a thorough reading within one or two seconds. Give yourself a couple of hours more flying time and you'll wonder how those guys in World War I ever managed with only a gas gauge, altimeter and compass—especially since none was probably very accurate or reliable!

The instrument panel on today's airplanes—even

on small training craft—tells you where you're going, how fast you're getting there, your altitude, how well the engine is performing and even how well (coordinated and smooth) you're making those turns. It's easy to see, then, why those once intimidating instruments quickly become respected friends. Without them you would simply be much less effective as a pilot.

The location of instruments on the panel will vary only slightly from airplane to airplane—although it seems long overdue for some sort of standardization among manufacturers. The Federal Aviation Administration has been working on such a proposal for more than a decade, but it appears it may well be that long in the future before you can expect to climb from a Piper Cherokee into, say, a Cessna 172 and find the instruments and switches in exactly the same place. It's a minor irritant, and one that most pilots have learned to live with but always grumble about. And perhaps rightly so.

Whatever their location, the following is a list of the flight instruments you'll use from the first moment you climb into an airplane as a student pilot.

ALTIMETER. This is the all-important instrument that tells you how far you and the airplane are above the ground. It is actually a sensitive aneroid barometer with the face calibrated and marked in feet rather than inches of mercury. As the altitude increases, the pressure decreases at the rate of about one inch of mercury for each thousand feet of altitude gain. Before takeoff a pilot should always set the altimeter at the field elevation. At most airports this information is posted near

The altimeter and barometric-pressure window must be set before each flight.

the runway at the point where you will stop for your pre-takeoff run-up and check. The altimeter usually has three pointers to indicate altitude. The long pointer indicates hundreds of feet, the middle-sized pointer indicates thousands of feet, and the thin pointer with the triangle-shaped end indicates tens of thousands of feet. When the 100-foot pointer makes one complete revolution, the 1000-foot pointer moves to one, or 1000 feet. When the 1000-foot pointer makes one revolution, the thin triangular-tipped hand will move to one, indicating 10,000 feet. Most altimeters now are equipped with a barometric-pressure-setting window (sometimes referred to as the Kollsman window) providing the pilot with a means to adjust his altimeter to compensate for the variation in atmospheric pressure. A knob is located at the bottom of the instrument for such adjustment.

AIRSPEED INDICATOR. This instrument usually won't register any speed at all until the airplane is moving at about 40 miles an hour or more. And that's okay since few if any airplanes will take off much under 70 mph. The airspeed indicator measures the *difference* between impact and static pressure. When the airplane is sitting still, these two pressures are equal. When the airplane moves through the air, however, the impact of the onrushing air is captured in the *Pitot* tube (under the left wing on the Piper Cherokee). This difference in pressure expands a small diaphragm inside the instrument and, through a mechanical linkage, moves a pointer to register indicated airspeed on the instrument face in miles per hour, knots or both.

Left: Airspeed indicator. Right: The vertical-speed indicator registers losses and gains in altitude more quickly than the altimeter but is almost useless in heavy turbulence.

The airspeed indicator will have green, yellow and red areas, indicating cruising, maximum maneuvering and never-exceed speeds.

VERTICAL-VELOCITY INDICATOR. Also called the vertical-speed indicator, this instrument simply tells you how fast you're going up—or down. It operates off pressure changes in the atmosphere and usually has a lag time of from six to nine seconds. Although valuable under normal flying conditions, during heavy turbulence, when altitude changes can be extreme and frequent, it becomes all but useless.

COMPASS. The magnetic compass was one of the first instruments to be installed in airplanes and is still the only direction-seeking device found in most general aviation aircraft today. It is always mounted on top of the instrument panel within easy view of both pilot and copilot or passengers. The airplane compass is simply a magnet with a face or card that enables you to read directions from zero to 360 degrees. Every 30 degrees, the compass has the number of that heading minus the 0. For example, 60 degrees is 6 and 240 degrees is 24 on the compass face. Compasses are aligned with magnetic north and not true north. They are also vulnerable to the motion of the airplane during turbulence and particularly steep turns, so a fairly comprehensive understanding of how compasses work, along with their natural limitations, is important in flying and will be covered in greater detail in Chapter 6 on navigation.

GAS GAUGE. There are two of these—one for each wing tank, and they operate the same as in your car.

The wise pilot, however, always makes a visual check of each tank before he leaves on a flight. Gauges of all kinds have been known to be wrong.

OIL-PRESSURE GAUGE. Every airplane is equipped with an oil-pressure gauge—and it can save you both trouble and money. Oil pressure should reach the normal operating value within 30 seconds during the summer and about one minute on colder winter days. During flight it should be checked every five or ten minutes, since it is the first indicator of oil starvation in the engine—which ultimately leads to engine failure and a forced landing. If oil pressure begins dropping, land as soon as is safely possible.

OIL-TEMPERATURE GAUGE. Another important indicator of the engine's internal condition during flight, the oil-temperature gauge also should be checked regularly. If the temperature climbs above normal, it means the cylinder heads are overheating, and serious damage and engine failure will soon result. Again, land as quickly as is safely possible.

TACHOMETER. This instrument is similar in many respects to the speedometer in your automobile. One end of a flexible cable is attached to the engine and the other is connected to the instrument. The rate of turning of the cable causes the expansion or contraction of rotating counterweights, and the engine speed is registered in revolutions per minute on the dial. On most small airplanes the propeller is connected to the engine crankshaft, so the tachometer registers both the engine and propeller revolutions per minute. You use the tachometer in an airplane more than most any

Tachometer. Redline is at 2700 rpm. Normal cruise range is between 2200 and 2400 rpm, depending on altitude.

instrument, since it is the only guide to power settings during takeoffs, landings, cruising and slow flight.

Gyro Instruments. Remember the little top you used to play with as a kid? A fascinating little toy that was actually a crude form of gyroscope. While the top was spinning, it couldn't be pushed over but would move parallel to its plane of rotation (the floor, most probably) in response to any kind of nudge. This action is called *rigidity in space.* Another characteristic of gyros is called *precession.* If a force is applied to the rim of a gyro while it is rotating, that force causes the gyro to react as if the force were actually exerted at a point 90 degrees around the rim in the direction of rotation. It is with these characteristics in mind that we discuss the use of gyro instruments in modern airplanes. Gyro instruments have played a major role in making instrument flight a practical part of aviation today, and

The gyroscopic heading indicator is more stable than the magnetic compass, but it must be adjusted every few minutes and possesses no direction-finding "brain."

it's important that the pilot understand how they work in order to use them more effectively.

DIRECTIONAL GYRO

OR HEADING INDICATOR. This will help you navigate without the magnetic dip errors and jumpiness in the regular compass. The heading indicator has no "brain" or directional finding abilities the way the magnetic compass does, so it must be set for a correct heading prior to takeoff and often adjusted periodically as you fly along. It is most useful to the pilot during turns and rough weather when the magnetic compass may lag or jump about. You couldn't fly by the DG alone, but it is a great aid to navigation and a helpful supplement to the compass.

ATTITUDE INDICATOR

OR ARTIFICIAL HORIZON. A miniature airplane and horizon on the face of this important instrument tell you the attitude of the airplane in relationship to

Left: Attitude indicator in level flight.
Middle: Attitude indicator in a climb.
Right: Attitude indicator in a descent.

the horizon at all times. It's one of the key aids to smooth and coordinated flight.

PICTORIAL TURN-RATE INDICATOR. In this instrument, a small aircraft silhouette rotates to show that the real airplane is banking, in which direction and to what degree. Also included in this instrument is the inclinometer, a curved glass tube with a small black ball resting in the center. By watching the ball a pilot can coordinate turns. When controls are properly coordinated, the ball will remain in the center position. Whenever the ball moves to the outside of a turn, it indicates the airplane is in a "skid," much like a car sliding sideways around a corner. If the ball slides to the inside of the turn, the opposite corrections must be made. Since the inclinometer ball indicates the need for more or less rudder, the general rule for student pilots is "to step on the ball." Gently, though. Airplane controls are sensitive and demand a light hand. Or foot, in this case.

Turn coordinator. When the wings of the miniature airplane are pointing at the bottom mark and the ball is centered, the pilot knows he is making a normal turn. At normal turn rate the airplane will make a 360-degree turn in two minutes.

Flying an airplane carries us into new worlds of experience and freedom. No longer are we confined to crowded city streets or hectic freeways. Our movement isn't inhibited by pedestrians, traffic lights and speed limits. We see the world from a new perspective—one that is private, picturesque and serene. But another part of the pilot's world is more demanding and disciplined, where each student pilot begins learning new traffic rules and speaking a different language. This is the airport.

2

The
Nerve
Center

Most of us have visited airports at one time or another, probably to catch a commercial flight ourselves or to meet friends arriving on one. In either case, the airport was most likely a large commercial operation with a busy terminal crowded with people, rushing around carrying luggage, checking schedules, waiting in lines, greeting or saying farewells to friends, relaxing in bars and coffee shops or browsing for souvenirs. Whether the airport was a large international center or a smaller municipal field, it was obviously a busy place that made you wonder how people stay out of each other's way long enough to get their job done. And yet most of the activity at an airport, such as ground- and air-traffic-control operations, goes on behind the scenes. The airport is the nerve center of aviation, and to the pilot, whether captain of a giant 747 transcontinental airliner or a single-engined Piper Cherokee trainer, an airport is a second home.

Once you begin learning to fly, airports will quickly be transformed from frantic, unfriendly centers of chaos to comfortable social centers where pilots relax and swap stories and anecdotes or share valuable information about such things as weather conditions. This is particularly true at smaller airports where most or all of the activity consists of general instead of commercial or military aviation. Sometimes these airports are as busy in terms of traffic as major commercial centers, but unlike the commercial airports, most of the people you find around general aviation centers are pilots or folks closely involved in some way with flying. You suddenly find yourself an enthusiastic member of a subculture you never realized existed.

There are more than 10,000 airports within the United States that serve all types of aviation. These range from awesomely large metropolitan airfields with several runways serving a variety of airplane traffic to refreshingly small grass strips suitable only for light airplanes. Airports are the places where flight training begins, and learning about airports and their operation is an important and integral part of that training.

A student's first encounter with airport operations will be taxiways, which enable airplanes to move to and from runways without interfering with airplanes tak-

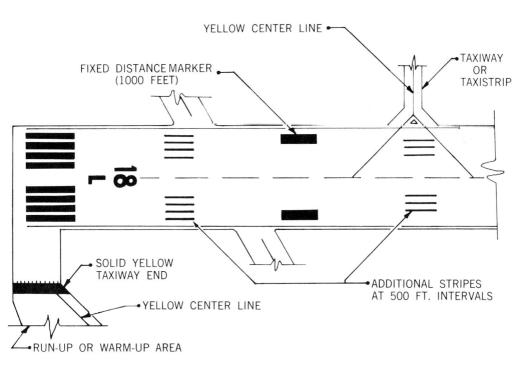

YELLOW CENTER LINE

FIXED DISTANCE MARKER
(1000 FEET)

TAXIWAY
OR
TAXISTRIP

18

SOLID YELLOW
TAXIWAY END

ADDITIONAL STRIPES
AT 500 FT. INTERVALS

YELLOW CENTER LINE

RUN-UP OR WARM-UP AREA

Taxiway and runway markings guide pilots during take-offs and landings and while taxiing to and from parking areas.

ing off or landing. These taxiways lead from the runways to aircraft-storage, tie-down, fueling and maintenance areas at the airport. Taxiways at most airports are marked by a narrow, yellow center line that guides pilots to and from parking areas. Wide yellow lines are used to indicate the end of taxiways where they meet or intersect with runways. These wider yellow lines indicate what is called "hold-short" positions where pilots can stop their airplanes for pre-takeoff checks and then must wait until they have clearance from the tower for takeoff or even to cross a runway en route to another. If there is no control tower, then each pilot is expected to wait behind these lines until certain there are no airplanes on a landing approach or takeoff run. Airplanes on a landing approach to an airfield *always* have complete right of way over those waiting for takeoff, or those taxiing to or from parking areas. A pilot should never cross an active runway at a controlled airport until the control tower gives clearance. At an uncontrolled field pilots must make sure there are no airplanes on a landing approach before crossing a runway. This, of course, demands strict attention.

Each runway at an airport is identified by a number determined from the magnetic direction of that runway. That magnetic-direction number is then rounded off to the nearest 10 degrees, with the final zero omitted. For example, a runway with a magnetic heading of 360 degrees on a northern heading would be identified as runway 36. That same runway, when a pilot is landing or taking off in the opposite direction, would become 18, since the pilot's heading would be 180 degrees —or south. This identification system for runways also helps pilots when they receive landing instructions from a control tower at an unfamiliar airport. When the tower instructs you, for example, to land on runway 18 (they'll say "one eight," but we will discuss radio jargon a little later), you automatically know what heading to use, or in other words, in which direction you will be landing even before you sight the airport.

The runway number is usually displayed on the approach end of each runway in large numerals that are easily visible from the air. The one- or two-number

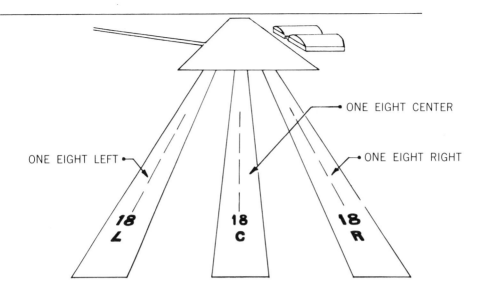

ONE EIGHT CENTER

ONE EIGHT LEFT

ONE EIGHT RIGHT

18
L

18
C

18
R

Runway heading markers aid both pilots and air traffic controllers.

system is used for two reasons. Using one or two numbers instead of three makes the runway name shorter and easier to say. Also, this permits larger numerals to be painted on the end of the runway, which goes a long way in making them easier to see from the air.

If there are parallel runways, they must still have the same number since their directions are the same. In order to identify each of them separately, a suffix letter is added to the runway number. For two parallel runways, the letters *L* and *R* would be used—indicating "left" and "right." If there are three parallel runways, the letters *L, C* and *R* would identify the left, center and right runway, each with the same heading number. For example, runway 36R.

It's important to keep in mind, however, that runway numbers are in relation to *magnetic north* and not *true north*, so the compass in the airplane should agree with the runway heading number—within plus or minus five degrees—when the airplane is aligned with that runway. Wind directions will also be reported by the control tower as part of the landing information so the pilot will have some idea of how much wind he'll be wrestling on that landing.

Wind is always a major factor in landings and take-offs. During these maneuvers, pilots should, as much as possible, fly directly *into* the wind. This is an ideal situation few of us ever encounter, however. Most of the time we struggle against a wind hitting from some angle that can rate as an irritant from mildly bothersome to maddeningly frustrating. Gusty winds can also be treacherous, but that primarily depends on the skill and attention of the pilot.

At controlled airports the tower will give you the wind direction and velocity. But there are several devices in use at most airports to help pilots *see* what direction the wind is coming from and also get an idea how strong and irregular it is. These devices, of course, are particularly important to pilots using uncontrolled airports.

The oldest and most common wind-indicating device is the *wind sock*. You'll find one or more of these at just about every airport around the world—whether it be a major commercial center or grass strip. The wind sock is nothing more than a cone-shaped device built of durable, flexible material open at both ends. When the wind blows through the large end of the cone, it causes the small end to stand out and point *downwind*. The amount of extension indicates how strong the wind is. A fluttering wind sock will warn a pilot that the wind is gusty—something he might not glean from tower information alone. Larger airports will usually have the wind sock illuminated at night so pilots can see it.

Another device in use at some airports is the *tetrahedron*. This wind indicator is a little more elaborate than the wind sock, and it is larger in size, which makes it easier to see from the air. The tetrahedron aligns itself with the wind flow causing the *pointed end* to

The traditional wind sock is still the most valuable and most common landing and takeoff aid to pilots.

Remember, the tetrahedron and the wind tee point in the direction the wind is coming from. *In other words,* upwind—*the direction in which the airplane should land.*

always turn *into* the wind, or upwind, which is just the opposite of the wind sock. The *wind tee* is shaped something like a miniature airplane and streamlines itself to the wind with the winglike structures facing upwind, just like the tetrahedron. At most airports you'll find a wind sock (or more than one) and either a wind tee or tetrahedron. Since most pilots are more familiar with the wind sock they find the wind tee and tetrahedron somewhat confusing. The best way to avoid that problem is to remember that both a tetrahedron and a wind tee point in the same direction that the airplane should land.

In addition to their numbering, runways may also provide other information to pilots that can be helpful during both landings and takeoffs. Some of them, usually at larger airports, may have a white center line to guide pilots, which can be especially helpful when visibility is bad, such as in fog or heavy rain.

White markings are also used if the *threshold* or touchdown point of a runway has been moved from the actual spot where the runway appears to begin. The threshold line is used to mark the start of the usable section of the runway, and a pilot should not land until crossing these marks. Most thresholds are displaced because of obstacles like trees, wires or buildings at the end of the runway that require additional clearance during a landing approach. Very often these obstacles appeared on the scene after the runway was built. Sometimes, however, the runway may have been extended as a safety factor for additional roll-out room when airplanes are landing from the opposite direction. Whatever the case, the markings are there for safety reasons and should be adhered to.

Overrun, stopway and blastpad areas of runways are marked with a chevron pattern—slanted, dashed lines assembled in V shapes. These areas are not structurally capable of supporting airplanes during landing and takeoff. The shoulders or edges of runways also are sometimes marked with the chevron pattern to indicate they aren't strong enough to withstand the stress of landings and takeoffs either. And if you spot a runway with large yellow or white Xs painted at each end —don't land. Those X markings mean the runway is closed and should not be used except in an emergency situation.

AIRPORT TRAFFIC PATTERNS

A pilot is always busiest during landings and take-offs. This is partly because of the demanding job at the controls and partly because the airspace then is the most crowded. It's for this latter reason that the Federal Aviation Administration has set down certain guidelines to follow when flying near airports and during takeoffs and landings.

As a student pilot you begin learning about airport traffic patterns the first day you go up on your introductory flight. The *upwind leg* is the airplane's flight path immediately following takeoff, up to the initial climb-out altitude which is generally between 400 and 600 feet. Your instructor will usually explain that the airplane should be flown on an imaginary line extending straight out from the runway without drifting to either the right or the left. No turns should be made until reaching the climb-out altitude. The *crosswind leg* is used usually when practicing touch-and-go landings, and follows a path 90 degrees to the upwind leg. The normal departure leg would be at a 45-degree angle from the upwind leg.

When nearing a controlled airport, a pilot radios that airport from about five to ten miles out and gives his position and informs the tower he is landing. The tower will then give him clearance, tell him which runway to use and what the wind velocity and direction are, and sign off by telling the pilot to "report downwind." Unless otherwise instructed, he then prepares

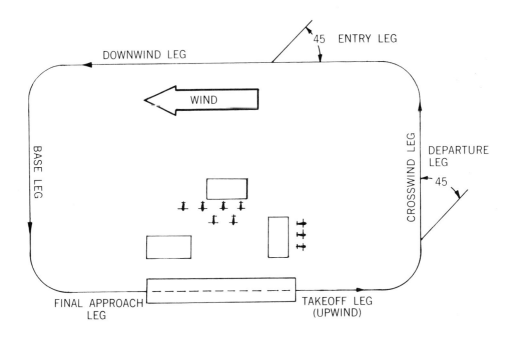

Typical airport traffic pattern.

for a left-hand pattern, which has become standard procedure at most airports.

The normal entry into the traffic pattern is to approach the *downwind leg* at a 45-degree angle approximately at the mid-downwind position. This approach gives the pilot a chance to check for any other traffic in the area that might also be entering the pattern. The downwind leg is flown parallel to the runway in the opposite direction from which the plane will be landing. The downwind leg also should be flown at the designated traffic-pattern altitude, which varies slightly from airport to airport, but is usually between 800 and 1000 feet.

The *base leg*—which runs at a 90-degree angle to the runway—begins at a point decided upon after you consider what other pilots in the pattern are doing, what the tower tells you, wind conditions and your own judgment and personal preference. On a "short approach" you may want to swing into the base leg about a quarter of a mile out from the end of the runway, or, if traffic is congested, you may have to follow a downwind leg that would carry you two or three miles away. Some pilots prefer short approaches, while others find that a longer final approach gives them time to align their airplane with the runway and set up for a smoother landing. During training, however, you'll probably be expected to learn both equally well in case you don't always have a choice—which is frequently the situation around busy airports. Being flexible about such things will also make you a better pilot.

The *final approach* is the path you follow straight in for touchdown. How you handle the airplane during this final few moments of flight usually determines how good a landing you'll make. You'll be busy making minor (but important) corrections, adjusting the power, feeling out the wind, checking the instruments, dropping flaps and generally drawing on every bit of skill and information you've ever picked up about flying an airplane.

And now for a word about courtesy . . .

Although there are rather specific guidelines for traffic in and around airports, there is still always room for simple courtesy on the part of everyone. Sometimes a number of other pilots may be using the traffic pattern practicing landings and takeoffs. If they all follow the normal spacing, it would be difficult and even dangerous for another airplane to try to enter the pattern. If a pilot sees someone trying to enter the pattern, he should extend his upwind takeoff leg and allow the other pilot time and room for entry. Likewise, if you are making touch and goes and see another pilot waiting a long time for takeoff, you could always pass up your next landing, or extend the downwind leg, and give him a chance to join you in the sky. A little courtesy like that is very much appreciated among the flying fraternity. As it should be anywhere else.

RADIO COMMUNICATIONS

Radio is considered by many experts to have contributed more to flying safety and a pilot's peace of mind than any other single development in modern aviation. At many airports today, use of the radio is as important to beginning a flight as starting the engine. The pilot talks first with ground control for permission to taxi and receives information on wind direction and velocity, altimeter setting and which runway to use for takeoff. Later in the flight, you will talk with the control tower for permission to take off, then proceed on a cross-country trip and periodically contact flight service stations along the route for weather and navigation information. Prior to landing, you contact the control tower for landing instructions and again are given pattern instructions, told which runway and heading to use on landing and given wind velocity and direction.

In short, radio communication has taken the guess-

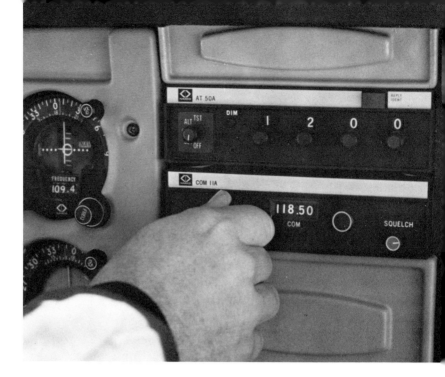

Tuning in control-tower frequency prior to takeoff. Most larger airports have a separate frequency for ground control and air traffic control. Frequencies are listed in the Airman's Information Manual.

work out of flying, and for those of us who have learned to fly in recent years, and in or near large metropolitan areas, it is all but impossible to imagine what aviation was like before such communication was available to most private pilots.

All student pilots are required by the Federal Communications Commission to have a restricted radiotelephone operator's permit. This permit may be obtained by filling out a brief application form, which will usually be provided by the flying school, and mailing it to the FCC in Gettysburg, Pennsylvania 17325. No experience or knowledge is necessary to apply for this permit, and it is valid indefinitely. In addition to your operator's permit—which you should *always* carry with you when flying—the airplane must also have a radio-station license on board. It's the pilot's responsibility to check the airplane's papers, so it's a good habit to develop early in your training.

Using the airplane's radio takes a little getting used to. My first few times up I found it annoying, even distracting, to have the radio blaring in my ear from the receiver speaker located overhead. But as my piloting skills improved and I no longer had to consciously *think* about so many things, I discovered I could listen to the radio almost subconsciously. As I began practicing touch-and-go landings and spending an hour or more in the traffic pattern, using the radio, listening to my instructions and keeping up with what others in the pattern or entering the pattern were doing, was not only necessary, but made me feel much safer and less lonely. I knew what other pilots were doing, and they, in turn, were aware of me. No guesswork. No frantic looks over the shoulder. Not that you don't have to stay alert and watch other traffic, it's just that the radio gives you a better idea of where that other traffic is and where it's going.

Most light training airplanes today come equipped with a hand microphone for transmitting and a speaker mounted somewhere in the cabin (above the pilot in the Piper Cherokee) for receiving. This setup eliminates the need for clumsy and uncomfortable headsets and generally makes for better reception. To use the mike you simply press a button, hold the mike close to your lips and speak clearly in normal conversational tones. It isn't necessary, as some student pilots seem to think, to yell or emphasize each syllable in a mechanical-sounding manner.

Be sure to depress the key or button before speaking, however. Otherwise, your transmission will never be heard or will be cut off midway if you release the button before finishing what you have to say. But it's important never to press the button on your mike or try to talk with the control tower when another pilot or the tower is transmitting on the same frequency, since that will cause what is called *cutting out* another transmission. All anyone can hear then will be a loud squeal.

I've found it to be a help to rehearse what I'm going to say before going on the air. One time after landing I switched to the ground-control frequency, picked up the mike and said: "Sonoma County Ground, this is Cherokee triple one Foxtrot Romeo, Redwood Aviation, taxi."

Parking area at Redwood Aviation at the Sonoma County Airport.

Ground control promptly came on and gave me permission to taxi—along with all the other information I would need for a takeoff—wind direction and velocity, altimeter setting and which runway to use. At first I was astonished. Then it hit me, and I was embarrassed. What I should have said was: "Sonoma County Ground, this is Cherokee triple one Foxtrot Romeo, taxi, Redwood Aviation." That way the tower would have known I had just landed and wanted to taxi *to* Redwood Aviation, instead of taxiing from there. But by merely reversing the words *Redwood Aviation* and *taxi*, I gave the wrong information, and, in turn, didn't receive quite the reply I expected.

Believe me, it was a painful experience to have to push that mike button again and explain what I really wanted. I could vividly picture the snickering expression on the guy's face in the tower. But I've never made that mistake again. And I bet I never will.

RADIO PHRASEOLOGY

As you gain experience at using the radio you learn to say just what needs to be said, without saying too much or too little. It may be difficult to understand what other people are saying on the radio at first, but it grows easier each time you fly. Part of the secret is knowing what to *expect* to hear. Most dialogue on the radio is very routine, and it's kept simple to eliminate any confusion and save time.

For example, when entering the downwind leg after initial radio contact with the control tower, a pilot would simply pick up the mike, wait until the frequency is clear, push the button and say something like, "Metropolitan Tower, Cherokee triple one Foxtrot Romeo, downwind."

There's no need for padding that with a lot of unnecessary verbiage like, "Metropolitan Tower *this is* Cherokee triple one Foxtrot Romeo *now on my* downwind *leg and ready for further landing instructions . . .*"

That doesn't mean that if you slip in a few ordinary conversational words that someone is going to jump on the radio and chew you out. Aviation isn't *that* rigid. But in flying, particularly while in traffic patterns, economy and clarity *are* important. Until you feel at ease with the radio—which may take 15 minutes or 15 hours, depending on you—think about what you need to say and rehearse it once either mentally or out loud before transmitting.

The pilot's world, in some ways, is a very small one. Within a few hours, an airplane can travel hundreds (and even thousands for large jets) of miles. And in certain parts of the world, such as Europe, international boundaries can be crossed several times in one day. To overcome the language barriers, the various countries of the world organized the International Civil Aviation Organization (ICAO) and adopted English as the international aviation communications language. This organization also adopted a phonetic alphabet to be used during radio transmissions, because many letters of the English language sound alike. For example, *B, C, D, E, T, V* and *Z* could all sound the same during a radio transmission.

INTERNATIONAL PHONETIC ALPHABET

A	Alfa (Al-fah)	**N**	November (No-vem-ber)
B	Bravo (Brah-voh)	**O**	Oscar (Oss-carh)
C	Charlie (Char-lee)	**P**	Papa (Pah-pah)
D	Delta (Dell-tah)	**Q**	Quebec (Kweh-beck)
E	Echo (Eck-oh)	**R**	Romeo (Row-me-oh)
F	Foxtrot (Foks-trot)	**S**	Sierra (See-air-rah)
G	Golf (Golf)	**T**	Tango (Tang-go)
H	Hotel (Hoh-tell)	**U**	Uniform (You-ne-form)
I	India (In-dee-ah)	**V**	Victor (Vik-tore)
J	Juliet (Jew-lee-ett)	**W**	Whiskey (Wiss-key)
K	Kilo (Key-loh)	**X**	X ray (Ecks-ray)
L	Lima (Lee-mah)	**Y**	Yankee (Yang-key)
M	Mike (Mike)	**Z**	Zulu (Zoo-loo)

Sometimes numbers also are difficult to understand in radio transmissions; therefore, they always should be enunciated clearly. Single-digit numbers are pronounced the same way as they sound except for the number *nine* which is spoken as *niner* in radio conversations. The ICAO adopted this substitute pronunciation because the sound of *nine* in German (spelled *nein*) means "no."

Multiple-digit numbers are generally spoken as single-digit numbers in series to avoid confusion. For example:

> 36—*three six*
> 795—*seven niner five*
> 0111—*zero triple one*

VHF and UHF radio frequencies are spoken as follows:

> 121.9—*one two one point niner*
> 118.5—*one one eight point five*

Round numbers up to 9000, such as those used for ceiling heights, flight altitudes and upper wind levels, are spoken in the following manner:

> 700—*seven hundred*
> 1400—*one thousand four hundred*
> 6800—*six thousand eight hundred*
> 9000—*niner thousand*

Numbers above 9000 are spoken by separating the digits preceding the word thousand. Some examples are:

> 10,000—*one zero thousand*
> 15,200—*one five thousand two hundred*

Airplane numbers usually are a combination of numerals and letters. For example:

> 111FR—*triple one Foxtrot Romeo*
> 7958G—*seven niner five eight Golf*
> 3752W—*three seven five two Whiskey*

Since altimeter settings always consist of two digits followed by a decimal point and two more digits, the decimal point is dropped when spoken. For example: 29.90 would be spoken as *two niner niner zero,* and 30.15 would be given as *three zero one five.*

24-HOUR CLOCK

To eliminate the confusion resulting from the 12-hour system of telling time, which is duplicated by the A.M. and P.M. method, a 24-hour clock is used in aviation just as in the military. Time is expressed in four-digit numbers. The first two digits indicate the hour and the last two figures represent minutes past the hour. Hours are numbered consecutively from midnight to midnight, from zero to 24. Some examples:

> 0000—zero zero zero zero (midnight)
> 0045—zero zero four five (12:45 A.M.)
> 0715—zero seven one five (7:15 A.M.)
> 1130—one one three zero (11:30 A.M.)
> 1200—one two zero zero (noon)
> 1420—one four two zero (2:20 P.M.)
> 1809—one eight zero niner (6:09 P.M.)
> 2259—two two five niner (10:59 P.M.)

Since a pilot in an airplane is often capable of crossing several time zones during a flight, a universal method of time was adopted to simplify the problems generated by time changes. The time used for flights, flight plans and communications is the time at Greenwich, England, a city located on the zero-degree line of longitude. This time is referred to as *Greenwich mean time* (GMT) or *Zulu time.*

Because the sun rises over Greenwich, England, when it is still dark in the United States, the time is always later when expressed in GMT or Zulu time than it is in the United States. To convert from local

SPECIAL RADIO PHRASES

Radio Phrase	Meaning
Acknowledge	Let me know that you have received and understood this message.
Affirmative	Yes.
Correction	An error has been made in this transmission. The correct version is . . .
Go ahead	Proceed with your message.
How do you hear me?	(Self-explanatory.)
I say again	(Self-explanatory.)
Negative	Not correct.
Out	Conversation ended and no response expected. The word *out* is rarely used, since it is usually obvious when the conversation is over.
Over	My transmission is ended but I expect a response. The word *over* is omitted if the message obviously needs a reply.

Radio Phrase	Meaning
Read back	Repeat entire message.
Roger	I have received all of your last transmission.
Say again	Repeat what you have said.
Speak slower	(Self-explanatory.)
Stand by	If used by itself means, "I must pause for a few seconds." If the pause is going to last longer than a few seconds, or if used to prevent another station from transmitting, it must be followed by the word *OUT*.
That is correct	(Self-explanatory.)
Verify	Check with originator.
Words twice	As a request: "Communications are difficult. Please say every phrase twice." As information: "Since communication is difficult, every phrase in this message will be spoken twice."

time, it's necessary to *add* the appropriate number of hours to the local time to determine GMT or Zulu time. To convert to Zulu (GMT) from:

Eastern Standard Time .... add 5 hours.
Central Standard Time .... add 6 hours.
Mountain Standard Time .... add 7 hours.
Pacific Standard Time .... add 8 hours.

Sometimes a pilot may wonder about the quality of his transmitter. If so, he can ask the nearest facility to give him a check by saying, "Radio check, please," or "How do you hear this transmission?" A reply will come back immediately that the transmission is "loud and clear," or "weak and garbled," or a reverse combination like "weak but clear." The first word describes the intensity or volume of the transmission and the second defines its quality. Sometimes the problem is with the radio in the airplane, or it could be the particular frequency. If other frequencies are available, it might be possible to improve transmission and/or reception by switching frequencies. If that doesn't help, the radio should be checked as soon as possible.

AIRPORT COMMUNICATION FACILITIES

At an airport that has a government (Federal Aviation Administration) control tower, a pilot is controlled by radio from the moment he leaves the parking area until departing the airport traffic area. At many major airports, *Automatic Terminal Information Service* (ATIS) is provided to give departing and arriving

The maintenance shop at Redwood Aviation. Most fixed-base operations offer complete repair and over-haul service.

pilots advance information on active runways, weather conditions, communication facilities and NOTAMs (notice to airmen) affecting the airport and pilots at a particular time. Where this service is available, it's a good idea to listen to this station prior to contacting any other radio facility on the field. ATIS frequencies are listed in the Airport/Facility Directory (Part 3) of the *Airman's Information Manual* (AIM) and are shown on sectional charts along with other pertinent airport data.

The next frequency used by the pilot (or the first in many cases) would be *ground control*. The ground controller is in the tower and is responsible for all traffic on the airport surface. A typical transmission to ground control would go something like this: "Metropolitan Ground, this is Cherokee triple one Foxtrot Romeo at American Aviation—taxi."

The ground controller would then come on the air, repeat your number, and give you whatever information was necessary. This will usually include which runway to use for takeoff, altimeter setting, wind velocity and direction, and then clearance for taxi.

After ground control, the next contact would be the *control tower*. Having completed the takeoff checklist, a pilot will then switch frequencies and ask permission for takeoff. Tower controllers are responsible for control of all airborne traffic—both arriving and departing—within the airport traffic-control area. When asking for takeoff clearance, that same pilot would say, "Metropolitan Tower, Cherokee triple one Foxtrot Romeo, ready for takeoff."

The normal response to takeoff requests is "cleared for takeoff." If the controller says, "Cleared for immediate takeoff," that probably means there is another airplane on a close final landing approach and he wants you to get moving. Or, in the same situation, he might instead tell you to "hold short for twin Piper on final approach." After the other airplane has landed, the controller will then clear you for takeoff by saying, "Cherokee triple-one Foxtrot Romeo, now cleared for takeoff."

In cases where there is considerable traffic, both landing and taking off, the controller might say, "Cherokee triple one Foxtrot Romeo, taxi into position and hold." This means he wants you to roll onto the runway, face the takeoff direction and then stop and wait until you receive clearance for takeoff.

Don't be afraid or reluctant to exercise your own

judgment, however. If you see another airplane on final approach and the tower has given you clearance for immediate takeoff, but you don't want to rush things, say so. Pick up the mike and say, "Cherokee triple one Foxtrot Romeo, we'll hold short for twin Piper." You may be guilty of holding up traffic for a minute or two longer, but no other pilot (especially the one landing) or tower controller will fault you on that. As the flying satire goes, "There are old pilots and there are bold pilots, but there are no old, bold pilots." And I believe it.

So now that you've been introduced to airplanes, airports and the language of pilots—let's go flying!

3
In
the
Beginning

The first step was simply to dial the telephone. Maybe my hand trembled a little and I had to clear my throat before I started talking in order to eliminate that nervous quiver I knew would punctuate my words. But I had finally made up my mind. I'd been living with excuses for more than a decade, and I'd finally run out of them. My schedule was probably never going to get any lighter.

Yes. This was the day I would begin to live what until now had been a fantasy since boyhood. Maybe it was a little foolish or hedonistic. But, dammit, I was going to learn how to *fly!*

"Good afternoon, Redwood Aviation," came the mellow female voice over the phone.

"Uh-*hem*, yes . . . I would like some information about taking lessons. I'd like to get my . . . uh . . . private pilot's license . . ."

"Oh, certainly," the voice said, and then calmly proceeded to give me brief information on what it would cost (about $1000) and how long it would take. "We'd like to invite you out for an introductory flight at your convenience. It will only cost you five dollars. You'll go up with an instructor and fly around for an hour and see how you like it. And when you come back down you'll already have an hour's worth of flying time for your logbook should you decide to continue on as a student . . ."

I didn't know what would happen during that first "introductory offer" as she called it, but I had already made up my mind about sticking with flying, and the five bucks was certainly attractive.

"Great. When can I start?" I asked.

"Just one minute, sir, and I'll check the schedule."

I hadn't expected that at all. Were they really *that* busy?

"Any time day after tomorrow would be fine," the voice said after a brief wait. "Can you make it then? Late morning or afternoon would probably be best. It's been a little foggy around here in the mornings . . ."

"Sure, that's fine. What about, oh, say, one o'clock?"

"Very fine. Now what is your name, sir?"

So that was it. My God! My first lesson already scheduled. The wait would be . . . agonizing.

When the moment finally arrived two days later for me to leave for the airport, I felt surprisingly calm. Maybe it still seemed like a dream. I don't really know what I expected. It was one of those warm spring afternoons when a few puffy white clouds drift lazily across a pale blue sky. My wife smiled and said, "Have fun," as I left. She seemed pleased that I was finally getting to do something she knew I had wanted to do for as long as she had known me. But otherwise she seemed very unimpressed about the whole thing.

As I headed north on the freeway, I looked skyward and spotted a couple of small airplanes circling in the direction of the airport. In a few minutes, I thought, I'll be up there, too. But right now I could be heading anywhere—the grocery store, a picnic, an interview. I'd driven to airports hundreds of times before, but always either to pick up friends and business associates or to catch a commercial flight myself. But somehow, driving there now to begin flying lessons didn't seem *real*.

I felt a strange mixture of enthusiasm and anxiety as I parked the car and headed for the office at Redwood Aviation. Feelings of doubt (Am I really cut out to be a pilot?), irresponsibility (Should a family man really take up something as frivolous as flying?) and even fear (They say it's safer than driving a car, but . . .) began creeping into my confused mind. I just kept walking—trying to appear as nonchalant as possible.

"Hello," I said to the smiling female face behind the counter. "I'm Monty Norris and I'm scheduled for an introductory flight this afternoon . . ."

"Oh, yes . . ."

A brief exchange of introductions followed as I met Steve Jones, one of the co-owners, a couple of instructors and then Phyllis Cantrell, an attractive blonde woman of about forty, who, I was informed, was chief flying instructor and my teacher—should I decide to continue lessons after my introductory ride this afternoon. I was handed some literature on flying and Piper airplanes, along with the Piper Instructional Program kit, which I was told would be my portable classroom for the next few weeks. The PIP, as I soon learned to call it, replaces the traditional ground school and is supplemented with cassette films and audio tracks that could be viewed on a machine at my own convenience in the office. Pretty nifty, I thought. Very streamlined.

"Okay, Monty," Phyllis said. "Let's go on out and introduce you to the airplane and then take a little ride."

Just like *that?*

Just like that.

We walked across a concrete ramp to a row of airplanes and stopped beside an orange and white Cherokee. My flying lessons began at that moment.

"The first thing you always do is climb in the cab and make sure the key is out of the ignition and the master switch is in the 'off' position," Phyllis said. She continued on through the walk-around external check, explaining the importance of each item in her friendly but serious manner.

Check the flaps and ailerons for any sign or indication they may be loose or otherwise not in top operating

Checking flap and aileron hinges is an important part of the visual external check of the airplane before each flight.

condition. Open the gas tanks to check the fuel level and look for signs of condensation. Water and gas don't mix. Then lean down and open the drain valve to let a little gas run out as a double check against water in the tanks.

Next, we opened up the engine cowling, and Phyllis explained some things about the 150-horsepower, four-cylinder Lycoming power plant, its dual ignition system and how before each flight the pilot should inspect the engine closely for any signs of oil leaks, cracked hoses and birds' nests.

"Birds' nests?" I asked.

Above: Check each fuel tank visually before a flight. Don't trust the gauges. Below: Checking the fuel tanks for water condensation is a must before every flight.

"Oh, yes," Phyllis said. "We just picked the beginnings of a nest out of that one this morning," she said, pointing to a twin-engined airplane down the line. "That's always a problem. The air ducts in the front of the cowling are an invitation to birds, I guess, but we're always picking nests out of the engines—just about every day. If you didn't check and there was a nest in there, it could damage the engine. Hopefully you'd find out about it before takeoff. But to eliminate *that* hazard we check first. Then you don't have anything to worry about!"

I got the message. Preventive medicine.

Always make a visual check of the engine before each flight and be alert to any signs of birds' nests. Warm airplane engine compartments are favorite camping sites of our feathered friends.

As we walked around the nose of the Cherokee, Phyllis stopped in front of the propeller to explain its role in the mystery of flight. The prop, she said, should always be examined, too, for any nicks that might indicate it had been damaged and needed replacing. Look around on the ground for any rocks or other objects that could be hurled backward by the prop wash and wind up hitting a person or another airplane.

We moved on around the airplane and opened the cowling on that side for further inspection of the engine, then moved on to the gas tank on that side, the Pitot tube and the stall warning device, knelt down and looked over the landing gear, inspected the lights, the tail assembly, including the rudder and stabilator, with Phyllis carefully explaining the function of each as we went along.

"There are specific things like this that you check each time," she said. "But in general you want to look the airplane over carefully for anything that might be wrong. Make sure the lights aren't broken, inspect the wings for dents—anything that might indicate damage. If you even have any doubts, have a mechanic or someone with experience take a look at it. That also protects you from being blamed for something you didn't do."

It all made sense to me, but I also was beginning to think flying must be pretty risky business to begin with, right? Maybe . . .

Before I had a chance to talk myself out of the introductory flight, Phyllis ushered me up into the cabin.

"You first," she said smiling.

The Piper Cherokee—which would be my training airplane—has dual controls, but I knew that the *pilot* always sits on the left-hand side. Why was *I* getting in that seat? I thought this was supposed to be an introductory flight. Didn't that mean I was just supposed to go up with my instructor and ride around to see if I got airsick or something?

Phyllis handed me a clipboard with a mimeographed sheet on it and began going over the starting checklist with me. The list seemed intimidating. So did the panel before me—a collage of dials and switches that looked much too complicated for a guy who has fits of frustration just trying to change a typewriter ribbon. Was I in over my head? The Piper Cherokee is a small, easy-to-operate airplane by today's space-technology standards. But to me it looked like nothing less than a Boeing 707.

We went through the starting list verbally:

"Seat latched."

"Seat belts on."

"Brake on."

"Fuel selector on."

"Mixture rich."

"Radio off."

"Master switch on."

"Electric fuel pump on."

"Check pressure."

"Fuel pump off."

"Prime as required."

The next item told me to "clear and start." Phyllis told me to turn the ignition to start, then press the key

Examine the prop for any nicks that might indicate excessive wear.

in slightly and when the engine turned over to release the key and give it a little throttle.

"But not too much," she warned. "You don't want to run the engine too fast right away. Let it warm up a little first. Maybe five minutes. Give the oil time to circulate some."

I cleared my throat and shouted, "Clear!" and started to turn the key that would pump life into the engine and begin my flying experience. But Phyllis grabbed my arm.

"You better say it louder than that. It's supposed to be a warning to people nearby that you're starting the airplane. You have to say it loud enough so people *outside* can hear."

"CLEEEAAAAR!"

"That's better. Go ahead."

I turned the key, and the propeller spun two or three times slowly before the engine groaned and rumbled into life and set the Cherokee to rocking and bobbing like a boat at sea. Phyllis took the microphone and muttered something I didn't understand. Then a voice boomed over the receiver, spitting out a series of numbers that left me blinking in confusion. Phyllis reached over, released the brake and told me in which direction to go. My surprise must have shown. Did she mean *I* was supposed to taxi the airplane out there? Yes, that's exactly what she meant.

"Steer with your feet," she said calmly. (Why did I expect her to be nervous?) "Left rudder (pedal) to turn left. Right rudder to turn right. Remember you've got wings now, so watch your clearance on each side."

Steer with my feet. Work the throttle by hand. Watch my wings. Whew! I hadn't even taxied out to the runway yet, and already I was in over my head! The gang in the control tower probably thought I was drunk the way I weaved along the taxiway.

Right rudder. Whoops! Too much. Correct it with some left pedal. Whoa!! A little more right. Not *too* much.

We stopped short of the runway, and Phyllis told me to face the airplane into the wind and begin my pre-flight run-up check, using the information on the clipboard and on the instrument panel.

Head into wind. Nosewheel straight. Brake on. Idle set at 800 to 1000 rpm. Primer locked. Altimeter set at field elevation. Gyros set. Run up engine to 1700 rpm. Check magnetos by switching ignition first to the right mag and then to the left one. There should be no more than a drop of 175 rpm—maximum. Push on carburetor heat and see that the engine doesn't drop more than 100 rpm. Throttle back down to 800 to 1000 rpm again. Switch to tower frequency and turn to checklist on dash: Electric fuel pump on. Fuel selector on correct tank. Door latch locked. Check. What now?

Phyllis handed me the mike. "Just say, 'Sonoma County Tower, Cherokee five six eight eight seven, ready for takeoff.' "

I did, and the tower controller's voice boomed back through the receiver above my head.

"Cherokee five six eight eight seven, cleared for immediate takeoff—Cessna on one-mile final."

Phyllis and I both looked up at the other plane on its final approach. She turned back.

"Tell him we'll hold short."

"Cherokee eight eight seven. We'll hold short."

"Roger eight eight seven."

The Cessna seemed to glide silently in and touched down gracefully on the runway. I gazed at it and wondered how many years it would take before I could produce a landing like that.

"Eight eight seven, cleared for takeoff on runway one niner."

"Eight eight seven—roger," I said boldly.

"Okay," Phyllis said. "Just ease the throttle all the way on and steer the airplane down the center of the runway. When your airspeed indicator reads about 70 miles an hour, the airplane will want to fly. Just ease back—smoothly—on the control wheel."

Seventy miles an hour? Steering with my FEET?

I pushed the throttle forward and the Cherokee responded with impressive acceleration. It seemed slightly easier to steer the faster we traveled—although I still weaved some. I looked frantically down at the dash, searching for the airspeed indicator. I couldn't pick it out in the maze of instruments, and I was afraid to keep my eyes off the road—er . . . runway.

"Okay, start pulling back on the controls. Steady pressure . . . that's it. A little more . . ."

The Cherokee lifted off. I was flying. Flying!

"We hold a straight line until we reach 600 feet," Phyllis was telling me. But my mind was on the blue sky in front of me and the rolling green hills and valleys spreading out below. "At 600 feet we make a 45-degree turn to the left . . ."

The rudder pedals, which had seemed hard to operate on the ground, now were so easy to work that I found myself overreacting, sending the Cherokee into bouncy skids to the left and then the right. I felt clumsy.

As we made a turn and headed toward the coast, Phyllis explained that for the first few lessons we would concentrate on straight and level flight and making turns while maintaining altitude. None of that sounded particularly demanding, but I changed my mind after

Left: The Pitot tube is a favorite camping spot for spiders. Make a visual check, but don't blow in it! That's a good way to break the airspeed indicator.

Right: This stall warning indicator on the leading edge of the wing activates a light on the instrument panel 5 to 10 mph before the airplane reaches actual stalling speed. It should be inspected before each flight.

making a simple turn and discovering that it was not only a little jerky, but I lost nearly 200 feet of altitude in the process.

We were up for about thirty minutes. It seemed like only about ten. Phyllis took over again as we returned to the airport and entered the pattern. I listened intently to what she said on the radio, and the response from the tower, but none of it made any sense. A lot of mumbo jumbo.

"Wind one two knots at two one zero . . ."

"Are you going to leave landing this thing up to me?" I asked with a note of panic in my voice.

"Just keep your hands and feet on the controls and follow what I do," Phyllis said.

The landing still made me a little nervous. Maybe it uncovered an old fear of falling that I didn't know was buried inside me. As she nosed the airplane down and cut back on power, I had a strong urge to reverse everything she was doing. But I resisted.

As the Cherokee settled closer to the runway surface, Phyllis worked the rudder pedals to keep it lined up, and then steadily pulled back on the control wheel until we felt the plane gently touch down.

I looked over and smiled at her as I let out a sigh. Safe again.

"Well, what do you think?" Phyllis asked as we left the airplane and headed back for the office. "Want to come out again?"

I smiled at her and nodded. "It's addictive, isn't it."

She smiled back. "Yes, it is. Shall we set up some lessons for next week?"

I said, "Beginning Monday."

SECOND LESSON

This was almost a carbon copy of the first day we went up. Phyllis reviewed everything from the first time, and I was surprised that I remembered a lot of it, although I had to labor through each item methodically.

Phyllis had me use the mike this time to call ground control and the tower for taxi information and takeoff clearance. I had a hard time understanding what they were saying. It's not that the guys in the tower don't talk clearly, it's just that what they said still sounded like mumbo jumbo. I mentioned this to Phyllis.

"That's normal at first," she said. "You don't know what to expect. But once you get used to hearing it and know what information they're going to give you, it isn't hard. There aren't but a few things they'll say."

I felt better hearing that.

It was a beautiful sunny spring day with a few cumulus clouds off in the distance on the horizon. Perfect for flying, I thought. We ran through the checks again, and it all seemed a *little* less confusing this time.

There's a thrill to getting airborne. I don't know if it will ever grow old. I hope not.

I felt a little uneasy at the controls. Sort of tense. I wanted to relax and I could feel myself overreacting. It was a very turbulent day, and that makes it hard to fly straight and level or make turns without losing altitude. For me, that is. I also have trouble working the trim tab and knowing when the plane is actually flying level. Phyllis reminded me that this takes practice and familiarity.

Time passes so fast up there. It's time to land before I really loosen up and begin to enjoy myself. The turbulence bothered me, but I figure it was good training.

As we started to land, another airplane, a Piper Comanche, which is faster than the Cherokee and has retractable landing gear, was coming in for a landing. Phyllis radioed the tower to let the Comanche land first. The tower relayed the information, and a sweet feminine voice came on and said, "Thank you, dear." The other pilot. It seemed refreshingly informal.

We followed the Comanche in for another smooth

landing. Same procedure as last time up. I followed Phyllis's lead with the controls. This time landing didn't seem so spooky to me, and I concentrated more on what Phyllis was doing than before.

I commented on the trickiness of landing to Phyllis after we parked the airplane, and she mentioned that landing is "when you put it all together."

I've got a long way to go yet.

THIRD LESSON

I make the external check by myself this time. Then review it for Phyllis as a double check. No problems.

Takeoff is still a little unnerving. I don't know why. But what a thrill. That may be the best part of flight

Don't forget to remove the chock blocks before starting the airplane and trying to taxi.

Tie-down chains must be released before starting the airplane and taxiing. Forgetting them would be an expensive mistake!

for me at this point. It's beautiful again today with a creamy fogbank rolling in from the coast about 10 miles west. Lovely sight, but Phyllis warns me to stay away from fog. That's the rule until you get your instrument rating. She doesn't have to worry. I wouldn't go near the stuff. She says we can fly *over* it, however.

I'm beginning to get more of a feel for the controls now, especially the trim tab. Made some 90-degree and 180-degree turns today without losing more than a few feet of altitude. Pride is stirring. Also set the plane up for landing and lined it up nicely for her. I'm feeling eager to take charge more. I wish I could fly about three or four hours each day, but she insists it would be too much to absorb. I know she's right. But I'm still eager.

FOURTH LESSON

It's sunny and warm today—perfect for flying. I flew the Cherokee up to 2000 feet, and then we headed toward the coast to practice some more turns. Climb to 3000 feet and then start the 90- and 180-degree turns.

Hold the nose up slightly to keep altitude. Watch the turn indicator. Coordinate the feet and hands. Get the right bank. Wind gusts coming in off the Pacific follow the rolling hills and make for some bumpy going— good training for a beginner, but a little frustrating. It's hard enough holding level altitude and coordinating those turns without having to cope with the turbulence. Ah, well. Excuses, excuses.

After a few turns, Phyllis tells me to straighten out and head back inland.

"Now I want you to bring your airspeed down to 90 miles an hour and maintain your altitude," Phyllis said.

What? Ninety miles an hour seems awfully slow. Normal cruising speed is around 110 mph. I'm wondering if the damn thing won't just drop out of the sky at ninety. I remember from one of several books I've been reading and the PIP that I should pull back on the controls to lift the nose and get the airplane in the right attitude. Too much nose-up attitude will cause it to stall eventually, but just enough will slow it down without losing that precious altitude. The ground looks awfully close, even though the altimeter reads 2000 feet. Oh well, here goes . . .

I pull back and the nose blocks out the sight of the horizon. The airspeed indicator starts dropping, but the altimeter indicates I'm climbing slightly. Too much power. Ease back on the throttle. Just a little. Drop the engine speed about 200 rpm. Yes! It's working! The airplane soars along quietly at 90—holding altitude. It really works. Another revelation.

FIFTH LESSON

There's a gray cloud cover this morning and a fog-bank is rolling silently in from the Pacific some 15 or 20 miles west. Rain is expected within the next couple of hours, but Phyllis and I will still have time for a few maneuvers. I head the Cherokee south toward Petaluma and make some more turns.

At about 1200 feet we hit rain. Phyllis calls the tower. No problem, she says. It's just good manners to let the guys in the tower know what conditions are. We'll stay under 2000 feet this morning and stick fairly close to home in case the weather closes in on us. Which it quickly did.

After about thirty minutes in the air we start working our way back toward the airport, but it appears engulfed in dark rain clouds. Visibility is down to about two miles. I'm glad Phyllis is with me—with her experience in instrument flying there won't be any danger. Flying seems strangely exciting in inclement weather. Rain is blasting the windshield, and the radio is alive with talk from other pilots arriving in the area who are surprised by the weather. I call the tower and ask landing instructions. Being up in this weather gives me a feeling of importance. A seasoned pilot employing all his skills—unperturbed by a little wind, rain and clouds. I line up the Cherokee on the final leg, and then Phyllis takes over for the actual landing, while I keep my hands and feet on the controls and follow through on her precise movements.

Back in the office, with a warm cup of coffee in my

hand, I feel as though I've just survived some sort of daring adventure.

SIXTH LESSON

A low ceiling again today with expected showers, along with a stiff wind out of the northwest. I'm getting the hang of these takeoffs now. Phyllis mainly sits back and watches. I climb to 600 feet and then bank to the left to leave the pattern. I'm starting to get more of a feel for flying now—which means, Phyllis explains, that I'm actually learning to fly the airplane and don't take a passive role as observer.

"Keep it at 1000 feet today," she says. "Just under the cloud cover."

I climb to 1000 feet and then level off and set the trim tab.

"Okay, now let's slow down and cruise at 80 mph."

Here we go again. Eighty seems so incredibly slow—especially at only 1000 feet. I mean, I can see carpenters pounding nails in a new housing project below!

I pull back on the controls and ease the throttle back for a lower rpm. Like magic. It works. The Cherokee settles back and quietly cruises along at a steady 1000 feet, the engine practically at idle.

"Okay. Fine," Phyllis says in something of a noncommital voice. "Now let's head east; I want you to practice circling a ground point. Just pick out something like a church or a big tree—something—and start circling it while maintaining your altitude."

Okay. I'll try. I spy a house with a large fir tree nearby. Looks like a good, visible reference point.

"Now keep the house and tree in sight and make wide circles," Phyllis explains. "Remember, you've got wind coming out of the northwest, so you'll have to compensate for it with proper wing attitude."

I make one circle and see right away that this business is tougher than I'd imagined. When the wind is hitting the underside of the plane perpendicularly, I have to lessen the angle of bank or be pushed off course. Everything keeps my mind, hands and feet busy: coordinate rudder and aileron controls for smooth turns, keep the nose up so as not to lose altitude, bank steeply on downwind turns and more shallowly when the wind is hitting the Cherokee at right angles. These turns would be a lot easier without the wind. But this is *good training*. I'm getting the feel of it. Not that I'm executing the 360s like a veteran. But I am maintaining altitude and turning some pretty fair 360s—even against the wind.

"Very good," Phyllis says.

Golden words that nourish the ego.

"Now let's try them in the opposite direction," she suggests.

Roll out, turn the opposite direction, circle the house with its big tree. This time we're going clockwise and for some reason it seems harder. I complain to Phyllis.

"It takes time," she says. "It's harder for you to see your reference point from over there. Just make a few more and you'll get used to it."

I do, and the turns start to smooth out. That infernal wind isn't helping though.

"Okay, let's head back. Radio the tower."

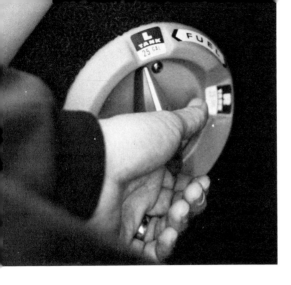

Making sure fuel selector is on fullest tank.

Another hour over already. They go fast.

I haven't landed the Cherokee by myself yet. Phyllis usually comes in and takes the controls on the final leg. But today she doesn't. At about three hundred feet up and a quarter mile out, I glance over out of the corner of my eye and see she is just *sitting* there. My feelings are bouncing around somewhere between sheer panic and a sense of excitement and pride. It's up to me now, and I'm going to show her I can do it.

The turbulence isn't helping, that's for sure. The damned airplane is wandering all over the place and it seems all I can do to keep it lined up with the runway. I start giving myself a mental pep talk. Maybe that'll help. I really want to pull this off.

Fifty feet off the ground now and nearly over the runway. By God, I've just about done it . . .

"Pull back now—*easy*—let it flare out. Keep the nose up and straight . . . pull back a little more . . . that's it . . . now keep that nose up even after you've touched down . . . keep the pedals even . . . you want that nosewheel straight when it touches down . . . there . . ."

Touchdown. Wow! Maybe it wasn't the most graceful landing in the history of aviation. But at least now
I know I can get an airplane up in the air, make a few
lazy turns, cruise along in slow flight and land it safely
(albeit a little wobbly). And that's one helluva lot for
a guy who couldn't even keep an airplane flying along
straight and level only a week before.

SEVENTH LESSON

Low-hanging cumulus clouds this chilly morning.
Another brisk breeze churning out of the northwest.
It's back to turning circles again—trying to cope with
the wind. The clouds force us to fly at 1000 feet.

Another attempt at slow flight. Reduce the throttle
power slightly, then ease back on the controls. Pull the
nose up. Watch the speed indicator. I'm beginning now
to feel that I can fly an airplane, even though my skills
are, at best, a little rough. Slow flight demands more
concentration and practice than I first thought.

Phyllis tells me I'm going to practice some S turns
next, using a road below to coordinate my turns and
use as a reference point.

Flying teaches you to become more aware of your
surroundings. Phyllis points out some ripples in a
small lake below.

"That indicates you have a pretty stiff wind coming
out of the northwest," she says. "You should always
look around and notice things like that. Now when
you turn into the wind you'll have to make shallow-
banks to stay on course. When you have a tail wind,

make the banks steeper or the wind will push you away from your reference point."

It's turbulent besides, but I'm beginning now to get a feel for coping with the turbulence and wind both. All the basics we've been working on the last few times out are starting to come together now. I still don't feel completely relaxed at the controls because of the concentration necessary. But even one simple turn I manage smoothly seems like a major triumph. I can almost feel myself learning and polishing my skills with each maneuver. And all those instruments facing me each time I climb into the airplane no longer intimidate me. I can glance over the panel and in a second know what the airplane is doing—or what I'm doing right or wrong.

The S turns are fun. As we advance into more difficult maneuvers, my enthusiasm grows along with a sense of accomplishment. A simple "very good" from Phyllis works like magic on my ego. What's more important, though, is that now *I* can tell when I'm doing well or having a bad time at it.

Time's up already. We head back to the airport, following the freeway below on a northern heading. I'm psychologically prepared for the landing this time, and as we cruise over downtown Santa Rosa, I pick up the microphone and radio the tower for landing instructions. I'm told to head on into runway 32, cutting across from the freeway, and to follow in the commuter airliner that has already been cleared for landing. Phyllis tells me to swing wide and head west, all the time watching for the other airplane. We finally spot it in the distance about three miles out.

The weather is closing in fast again. Rain is pelting the windshield, but visibility is good. At least five miles. I bank toward the runway and reduce power, then push forward on the controls to begin the descent. The small commuter plane is about a mile ahead and several hundred feet lower. It's a strange sight to follow another airplane in for a landing. Very difficult, for me at least, to tell how near or far it is to the runway. Or even when it is about to touch down.

"Okay, cut back the power a little more," Phyllis says. "You're a little high."

Cutting the power and dipping the nose still spooks me a little. But I feel much more relaxed about this landing than the one yesterday. Much more. We're about 100 yards out now and not more than 200 feet high. I'm not having as much trouble keeping the plane level today, even with the turbulence that has buffeted us all morning.

"Not too much back pressure yet," Phyllis reminds me. "Just look out at the end of the runway to get oriented. That's it. Fine. Now pull back on the controls just a little bit and drop the power again some more. Just a little. Pull back."

Touchdown! And pretty smooth too. Landing is the most magnificent feeling yet. As Phyllis said yesterday, landing is when you put everything you've learned all together.

A few minutes later, after I've parked the Cherokee and we're reviewing the day's workout, Phyllis says: "I've had people come out here and say they didn't want to learn how to fly, they just want to learn how to *land*. What they don't realize is that you can't land an airplane until you've learned to fly it."

EIGHTH LESSON

Bad day, today. Can't get anything together. Wind gusts made a shambles of my takeoff. I had drifted off the runway before I'd climbed 100 feet. Spent the day practicing slow flight, mostly. I would probably have been better off taking a nap or spending the afternoon working in the garden or perched on a stool at the nearest watering hole, I think.

I'm tired today. Phyllis eased some of the pain of making a bad showing.

"You've got to be alert. When you're tired or in a bad mood—that fouls your concentration, causes you to make mistakes."

Indeed.

NINTH LESSON

Takeoff is *perfect*—in Phyllis's words. I know it too, but it sounds so beautiful coming from her.

It's a gorgeous day. I feel great, and my flying shows it. We practice slow flight some more, make a few turns and bring the Cherokee back home for a dandy landing. A great note to end the week's training on—and a fine way to start a bright, sunny weekend.

TENTH LESSON

Landing-pattern practice today. We're using a former Navy training field now used only by a few private pilots. Landings are tricky. I have a tendency to come in too high and with too much power. Phyllis wants me to come in for a landing, but instead of actually touching down, cruise along the length of the runway about 15 or 20 feet above ground—or at whatever altitude I feel comfortable. This is to build landing skills and learn to control the airplane in *very* slow flight. I keep remembering her words about landings being the sum total of all your piloting skills. Mine don't add up to much yet.

The controls seem so mushy at landing speeds. I have trouble keeping the wings level and even lining up with the runway. I get a bit frustrated, but this is the most fun I've had yet. Each landing gets a little (very little) better. I can tell I'm fighting the airplane. Phyllis tells me to relax and take charge.

"I guess I'm too passive, huh?" I reply.

Phyllis nods. "I was, too," she says. "My instructors used to get on me continually for not being more aggressive."

There's such a fine line between taking charge of the airplane with finesse and manhandling it. You can't do the latter, nor can you play a passive role. A pilot really has to fly an airplane. That's part of the thrill and satisfaction of the whole experience. I have to work on that more.

I'm making some progress, though. I can remember

back a few days ago when even holding the airplane in straight and level flight seemed like such a challenge—turns demanded every bit of my concentration and energy. Even *taxiing* out to the runway was a struggle. I think part of the satisfaction of flying must be the learning experience itself—continuously building skills, then looking back with amusement and pride on how far you've come along. Right now I still feel humble. I even get a little embarrassed when I return to land with my many approaches—wings bobbing, and those bouncing touchdowns. I always expect the ground controller's voice to be chuckling when I get on the horn for taxi instructions. But it's always the same monotone.

I'm tired from the landing practice—physically and mentally. Phyllis is right about me struggling with the airplane. I can feel it in my back and neck muscles. Yet it isn't an unpleasant experience. It's odd how even mental fatigue can be relaxing.

LESSON ELEVEN

Practiced some more landing patterns today. Some improvements. I recalled Phyllis's words about landings: "That's when you put it all together."

For sure. Forget those Hollywood thrillers about the man or woman who can't fly, but lands an airplane safely while the guy in the control tower calmly talks them through it step by step. Maybe it's *possible*—but I wouldn't want to be one of the passengers. Too many things you have to know first. The controls get mushy

Setting the altimeter to ground elevation.

and the plane wants to yaw and skid, the wings dip, and it's tough trying not to overreact while making continual corrections. But it never gets *boring*. Believe me.

LESSON TWELVE

More landings and takeoffs again today. Perfect weather for flying despite a pretty stiff wind out of the west. Phyllis suggests we stay at home base for a touch-and-go session this time. Besides, it will give me valuable practice landing at a fairly busy airport and listening to and talking with the control tower.

Things went well. Especially the last two or three landings. I'm getting a feel for it now. Working the throttle and keeping the wings level, watching the airspeed, lining up the Cherokee with the runway by working the rudder.

"It never really gets *easy*," Phyllis said. "It just gets to be more fun as you get better."

And she's right.

I'm learning to set it down gently by pulling back just slightly on the controls. I have a tendency to want to yank back just before touchdown. Phyllis tells me this is a fairly common reaction among student pilots. Dropping to the ground at 80 or 90 miles an hour, you want to pull back just before touchdown to avoid hitting too hard. She told me to pull back just enough to keep the nosewheel up so that the airplane won't hit on it first. I finally did it, and the Cherokee settled down smoothly. I felt, first, a sense of surprise, then almost overwhelming pride when Phyllis looked over and said, "Beautiful."

LESSON THIRTEEN

More landings today. All weekend I've been practicing them—in the shower, at the dinner table. They were all perfect, of course. Or nearly so. And if something went wrong, I could stop in midair and start over.

A lot of crosswind action today. You really notice this most about 50 feet off the ground when you begin struggling more with the controls to keep the airplane headed straight in and the wings level. I'm also having trouble remembering to pull back on the controls after touchdown. It seems the minute the wheels hit the ground I relax the controls. Have to keep that nose-wheel off the ground until the airplane slows down some. Phyllis keeps telling me and telling me. Finally, after about half a dozen touch and goes I get it right. There are just so damned many things to think about on landings, and I'm really concentrating on setting the Cherokee down smoothly. I still have a strong tendency to overreact to the controls—even after a touchdown. Gets frustrating. But Phyllis says things are going well. I know I enjoy it more every day.

LESSON FOURTEEN

Rocky times in the airplane today. Just when I thought I was polishing my skills to an impressive

Setting the heading indicator prior to takeoff. You'll have to adjust this instrument every so often during flight, since it doesn't have a "brain" like the magnetic compass.

luster—Wham! I get hit with some nasty crosswinds.

"Good training," says Phyllis.

"I hope so," I muttered.

Good training, perhaps. But awful frustrating. On my first landing I was coming in on the final leg, pretty well lined up with the runway. Right altitude. Correct airspeed. Flaps dropped one notch. Throttle back all the way. Everything seemed fine. Then—*wham! whoosh!*—the runway seemed to move ... no ... jump ... to the right about 50 yards. Yeeee Gods! I banked the Cherokee and gave it full right rudder. Nothing. The airplane turned and banked but wouldn't line up with the runway.

"What the hell ..." I muttered.

"Pretty strong crosswind," Phyllis said. Sounded like a note of humor in her voice. It didn't seem funny to me.

I said: "Yeah. I hope so."

Here we are, about 50 feet off the ground, cruising along at about a 30-degree bank, dropping down on the runway nearly sideways, and nothing I do seems to make any difference.

"Line it up. Straighten it out," says Phyllis calmly. "Gently, though. Don't overreact with the controls."

Sure. It sounds so *easy* when she talks about it.

After what seemed like an exhausting and frantic struggle with the controls, I finally got the Cherokee straightened out about 15 or 20 feet off the ground, then pulled back on the controls to flare out for the touchdown.

Nothing. What the hell? There we were, cruising

along the runway—almost at stall speed—and the damned airplane wouldn't *land*. I pushed the control wheel in slightly to point the nose down. Down it went. Too much. Pull back. Up we go.

"Oh, come on!" I snapped, my frustration was showing.

Then the Cherokee settled down to earth (less than gracefully), and I started weaving down the runway, struggling with the rudder controls in what seemed like a futile effort to follow a straight path. Finally getting the Cherokee on a straight line again, I shoved the throttle in slowly and settled back, a little exhausted, for another takeoff.

"Now you know you're going to have to overcome a pretty stiff crosswind," Phyllis was saying as we reached 600 feet and banked right to enter the right-hand landing pattern again. "Don't overreact to the controls. And keep looking out at the end of the runway as you settle down to the ground. Just ease back— *slowly*—on the controls for your flare-out. And *keep* pulling back after you touch down."

I have to keep talking to myself to remember that. For some reason, as soon as the Cherokee touches down, I push the controls forward, which lowers the nose. But I've got to get out of that habit, because you want to keep that nosewheel up until the speed drops. Keep pressure off it. One reason is that if the airplane goes airborne again—which they often do—even for a few feet, you might come down the second time on the nosewheel, which isn't designed to support the full weight of the airplane. That also might jam the prop into the ground—which could prove both expensive and, possibly, disastrous. You want to keep the weight of the airplane off that nosewheel until you lose most of your airspeed.

The next landing wasn't any easier. The wind kept pushing me off the final leg, and each time I'd nearly touch down, a gust of wind would pick the airplane up again and I'd have to wrestle it to another bouncy landing. None of them were really *rough*, exactly. Just not what you'd call *smooth*.

Halfway through the lesson I had sweat running down my forehead and my back was getting tired. I knew this was mostly from not relaxing, but how could I relax when the airplane seemed to fight everything I wanted to do for it?

An ungrateful beast, testing the limits of my patience. Not to mention my still unpolished skills. (I was beginning to feel sorry for myself. Sort of the old "Lord knows I'm trying" rationale.)

None of the landings today were anything to brag about. Once, on my final approach, following in a high-winged Cessna, the tower ordered me to abort the landing since it didn't look as though the Cessna would clear the runway in time for us to take off again. I reached for the radio to roger their instructions, but Phyllis grabbed the microphone away from me.

"Hit the throttle and *go!*" she said. "They don't expect you to chat with them at a time like this. You've got more important things to do."

Right.

I went home physically and mentally tired that day,

but I learned more, I think, than in any other session to date. None of the landings were very good or graceful. But none of them were embarrassingly bad or rough on the airplane. After we had the airplane safely parked, Phyllis and I talked about crosswind landings, which until now had been merely some vague element of flying I remembered hearing about on the PIP or in reading.

"Dip the wing that's in the crosswind," Phyllis said. "If the wind is coming from the right, drop the right wing. Sometimes you may have to give it a *lot* of opposite rudder.

"It's all part of learning a feel for the airplane. Landings aren't easy. And no two are ever exactly alike. You have to approach each one a little differently. You're starting to develop a feel for the airplane, but you have to work on not overreacting. Make your corrections a little slower. You know what corrections need to be made now, you just need to practice until you're more consistent and smoother. It's going very well, though."

I only knew I was tired. Very tired.

LESSON FIFTEEN

Flew with the hood on today. It's something like a long visor that blocks out your vision except for the instrument panel. Flying by instruments only is a strange feeling. Phyllis says it's important because it teaches a student pilot more coordination and also prepares you for getting caught in nasty weather, clouds or fog. I put the Cherokee through a few 90- and 180-degree turns, some slow flight and some climbs. I can see what she means. Watching the turn indicator and altimeter forces you to really coordinate your movements.

After about fifteen minutes or so of this, Phyllis said she wanted to fly over an apartment house that had exploded about an hour earlier. It was a terrible sight. I circled at 1000 feet as we looked at the rubble and watched the firemen and police scurrying around. Then it hit me. Here I was, doing perfect turns around a point and not even thinking much about flying the airplane beyond occasional glances at the altimeter. Just a week or so earlier these same maneuvers would have demanded all my attention. I really have progressed!

LESSON SIXTEEN

Back to touch and goes again today after a week's layoff because of the flu bug. I'm a little rusty, but it feels good to be back flying. Still having some trouble on the final flare-out for some reason. I have a tendency to pull back on the controls too soon before touchdown, which causes the Cherokee to stall and drop prematurely, or else keep flying down the runway— depending on the wind and my airspeed.

I feel comfortable now flying in the traffic pattern and using the radio. It isn't even necessary for me to actually *listen* to the radio anymore, I seem to hear what's being said automatically.

The landings are getting better. I just need to polish my skills and make smoother corrections.

"*You're* flying the airplane," Phyllis said after I pulled off one fairly good touchdown. "Don't land it until you're happy with the way it's set up. You've got 5000 feet of runway here. Use whatever you need to land. There's no rush. And if you don't like an approach, go around again."

The next time around I held it off until everything seemed to feel just right, then pulled back gently until the Cherokee settled smoothly down on the asphalt.

"Perfect!" Phyllis said. "By golly, I think you've got it."

Later, as we climbed out of the airplane and walked back to the office, Phyllis said: "I think you're ready."

"Ready?"

"Yes. To solo."

I just grinned and listened to my heart pounding.

4
Going
It
All
Alone

So what's all the fuss about soloing? Nothing, really. Except to the student pilot it's a major step psychologically.

Or maybe I should have said *hurdle*.

The idea of soloing to the student pilot inspires all manner of strange emotions—pride, fear, excitement and anxiety. Usually all at the same time.

Why? Because it means that your instructor believes you have reached a level of proficiency in piloting an airplane, and that you can be trusted to take off, fly about some, return to the airport, contact the tower, enter traffic and land—all by your lonesome.

And it *can* be a lonely feeling.

My turn came on a Monday—an unlikely day in my life. Mondays have never been my favorite day. I'm what you could call a slow starter. I kind of like to ease through Mondays with as few challenges as possible. Sort of size things up for the week to come, so to speak.

I had pretty much forgotten Phyllis's parting words the Friday before my Big Day. Maybe it was a case of selective forgetting. I'm not sure. Anyway, I knew my solo flight was coming up soon, and I'd lived it in my mind over and over again now for at least a week. Phyllis had said she was reluctant to send me up on a really windy day, but otherwise I appeared ready.

I *wanted* to be ready, too. I felt I was. But . . .

It was warm that Monday. Pleasantly warm. No wind gusts. Only a slight crosswind drifting lazily in from the Pacific. I asked the tower for permission to take off and stay in the pattern for touch-and-go landings. The tower cleared me, and the Cherokee rolled down the runway, picking up speed and then gracefully soaring skyward as I pulled back on the controls. There was a little turbulence, but nothing uncomfortable.

"We're beginning to get some of our summer thermals," Phyllis said matter-of-factly after one bouncy encounter with those disturbing invisible chuckholes in the sky. I had just reached the pattern altitude of 1000 feet and reached up to ease back on the throttle to level off. We hit the thermal at that moment, and the bounce jostled us enough that I jammed the throttle back to full power.

"Good grief!" I muttered.

"Sometimes it gets pretty rough," Phyllis said. "One summer day it was so rough stuff was spilling out of the ashtrays. That's when you wonder what you're doing up here."

Yes.

I turned into the downwind leg and contacted the tower: "Cherokee triple one Foxtrot Romeo, downwind."

"Cherokee triple one Foxtrot Romeo, you're second to land behind the twin Cessna now on two-mile final."

"Triple one Foxtrot Romeo, roger."

I squinted into the fading afternoon sun and at the gently rolling hills of northern Sonoma County, scanning the horizon for the twin Cessna. There it was, about 200 feet below us. I waited until it had crossed my left wing and then I banked into the base leg, reduced the power to about 1700 rpm and pulled on a notch of flaps.

"Triple one Foxtrot Romeo, cleared for touch-and-go landing," the tower voice crackled over the radio.

"Triple one Foxtrot Romeo, roger," I responded.

I banked the Cherokee smoothly into the final leg, checked my airspeed and altimeter. Everything looked good, felt good. I seemed very much at ease today; in command of the airplane. Amazing for a Monday.

I knew before we even reached the runway it was going to be a good landing. Without those gusty crosswinds to battle, the airplane seemed surprisingly graceful and responsive. I added a bit of power to avoid touching down sooner than planned. Cut power. Eased back on the controls. The nose wandered to the left some. A little right rudder. Not too much. Don't over-control the airplane. Drop the right wing slightly. Ease back on the control wheel. Just a little more. *Touchdown!* So gentle you could barely feel the wheels settling onto the asphalt.

"Beee-*uu*tiful!" came the excited response from Phyllis.

I grinned modestly. "Thanks." (What else could I have said?)

"Okay, let's go around again and see if that was skill or just luck," Phyllis said.

I smiled to myself. Somehow I knew the next landing would be just as good. It was just one of those days. It couldn't be *Monday*.

Another circle and smooth landing. No better than the first, but just as good.

"By golly, I think you've got it." Phyllis chuckled.

"Looks that way," I said, big grin growing bigger.

I noticed Phyllis when she reached for the mike and said something briefly, but I was already busy putting full power to the Cherokee and guiding it down the runway for another takeoff. We were about a hundred feet off the ground when she did it—reached over and cut the throttle back to idle. The Cherokee seemed to hang motionless in space for a few seconds as my mind tried to catch up with what was happening.

"Put the nose down so you don't stall," Phyllis barked at me.

I realized then what she had done and why. Emergency procedure. What to do if you lose power on takeoff. I remembered Phyllis's answer when I asked her that question a week or so earlier.

"Look for someplace soft," she said.

Now I *was* looking for someplace soft. Only there wasn't anything below but that hard asphalt. Coming up fast. I nosed the Cherokee over until low enough to the surface to flare it out and land. Bump. Back down again. Not even a bad landing, either.

That was my first taste of emergency procedure. It wasn't as hairy as it would have been if I hadn't been over the runway, but it gave me some idea of what to expect and how to cope with a sudden loss of power at low altitude.

"The important thing to remember," Phyllis explained as we took off again, "is to immediately look for a place to land and get the nose down so you don't stall. You won't have time to turn around and come back to the airport."

The Cherokee climbed steadily (and healthily) to 600 feet as I mulled this information over in my mind.

"Okay, let's make this a full stop," Phyllis said, handing me the mike. "You don't need me any more."

"What's that mean?" I asked.

"I'm going to let you solo—unless you don't want to."

There was note of humor in her voice. Or was it sarcasm?

"Feel like you're ready?" she asked.

I swallowed. "Sure. I think so." Pause. "Yes."

"Good. Just do three touch-and-goes this time. That'll give you a chance to get used to being all alone before we have you fly out of the pattern."

A feeling somewhere in the twilight zone between sheer panic and total delight rushed through me. In a few minutes I'd be up here again—*alone*. Sure, I'd been flying now for a couple of weeks with only some coaching from Phyllis. But . . . all alone? What if . . . ?

"Just drop me off at the office and I'll sign your medical certificate. You did get your physical, didn't you?"

"Yes."

"Do you have your certificate with you?"

"Yep, right here," I said as I pulled the little yellow card out of my wallet and handed it to her.

She signed it and handed it back. "Okay, I'll be listening to you on the radio, so if you have any trouble or questions, don't hesitate to tell the tower, and we'll help you."

I nodded.

"Okay," Phyllis said as she climbed out, "we'll see you in a little while. Have fun." Then she shut the door and latched it. I was on my own.

I'm not really sure what I expected to feel, but a mellow calmness settled over me at that moment, mixed with a bit of pride and a sense of responsibility. About the way I felt that Friday night many years ago when my dad let me take the car alone for the first time. Something like that. Anyway, all those sensations of doubt, anxiety and even excitement—vanished.

I picked up the mike and asked for taxi clearance. It came, and I headed out to the runway for my preflight run-up. I faced the Cherokee into the wind, pulled the brake on and began running down the checklist. Then, I went over it once more just in case I'd overlooked something. There wouldn't be any Phyllis sitting there as backup for my blunders. I switched to tower frequency and then reached for the mike.

"Cherokee triple one Foxtrot Romeo, ready for take-off and touch-and-go landings."

I'm not sure, but I think I held my breath until the answer came over the radio. It seemed like at least three minutes.

"Cherokee triple one Foxtrot Romeo, cleared for touch-and-go landings. Report downwind."

"Triple one Foxtrot Romeo, roger."

Mike back in the clip. Release the brake. Ease the throttle forward. *This is it.* The Cherokee moved slowly toward the runway. I glanced over the instrument panel once more. Everything okay. I eased the throttle all the way forward now and watched the airspeed indicator moving toward 70 mph. Pull back gently. It was as if this were the first flight and Phyllis was coaching me through each and every move. I had to be methodical. This was not the time to miss *anything*.

There are old pilots, and there are bold pilots...

And then lift-off. I looked around me: down at the airplanes and hangers below, the freeway, rolling hills.

And the empty seat to my right.

For the first time since I had started flying lessons, I really felt like, *believed,* I was a pilot.

At 600 feet I banked and turned left into the crosswind leg. When the Cherokee reached 1000 feet, I cut back to cruising speed and entered the downwind part of the pattern.

"Triple one Foxtrot Romeo, downwind," I said in my smoothest Sky King voice.

"Triple one Foxtrot Romeo, cleared for touch-and-go."

As I entered the base leg, cut back the power to 1500 rpm and pulled on a notch of flaps, I wondered if my sense of calm self-confidence was really warranted or a bad case of blissful ignorance. But it was only a flash thought. As long as I concentrated on what I was doing and didn't let my mind grow cluttered with self-doubts and other mental confetti, why should these touch-and-go landings be any different from the ones I had been doing so well only a few minutes ago? No reason. End of conversation.

(I frequently give myself pep talks in times of crises.)

Keep that nose down, I told myself. Add power if you need it. And don't land if everything doesn't feel right. Watch that airspeed. One hand on the throttle. Don't try to touch down too soon. Cut the power. Ease back now on the controls. Easy. That's right. Just a little more. Not too much! That's better.

Touchdown.

I grinned. It almost turned into a giggle.

Now back on the throttle. All the way. Watch the airspeed indicator. Pull back to rotate the wings. And up we go again.

On the third go-round I told the tower I'd be making a full stop. I'd been at it alone more than twenty-five minutes, but it seemed more like five.

Back on the ground and taxiing toward my parking spot, I wondered what all the fuss about this solo business was. Nothing to it, really. It wasn't until I had parked and shut down the Cherokee that I realized sweat was running down my forehead and back so much it felt as though I'd just stepped out of the shower. (It does get pretty warm in those airplanes.)

Phyllis walked out to greet me wearing the biggest smile I'd ever seen on her.

"Congratulations. How'd it go?"

"Great."

"You sounded calm on the radio."

"I was."

That evening at the dinner table, my wife leaned over, and with a tolerant smile, said: "I'm very proud of you, but will you please land that airplane now. You're food's getting cold."

5

Polishing
Your
Skills

Once you've made that first solo flight, your self-confidence grows tremendously. You now feel like a real, honest-to-gosh *pilot*. You've taken off, flown about some and landed all by yourself. It's proof to friends and family that you can really fly an airplane—even if you aren't yet authorized to take them for a ride.

Now the fun and hard work begin.

"It'll go pretty fast from here on out," Phyllis said after my first solo experience that wonderful Monday afternoon. "I want you to get in some solo time now practicing the maneuvers we've been working on the past couple of weeks. After you've logged some solo time, and worked on some of those maneuvers, then we'll get ready for cross-country trips."

Polish my skills, huh? I really looked forward to going up alone—it would be my first chance to do what I really wanted, to enjoy the view and the serenity that comes with flying. But before Phyllis turned me loose to practice S turns across a road, and turns around a point (which she indicated would be important on my flight test), she went up with me one afternoon to practice "emergency procedures." The idea made me feel less than enthusiastic. There was something about the word *emergency* at this stage of my training that aroused feelings of inadequacy and butterflies in the stomach.

We flew south a few miles to a predominantly rural area of lazy rolling hills dotted with trees and cattle. She told me to fly at 1000 feet and look over the area closely for a possible emergency-landing sight.

Nothing down there looked even remotely inviting, and I was about to tell her that when she reached over, pulled back on the throttle and said, "Power failure, forced landing." I pulled back gently on the control wheel to reduce my airspeed and put the Cherokee in a glide, just as the textbook in my Piper kit had explained. Then I began hastily scanning the area below. A pasture about two miles away, nestled in a valley, looked like the best choice. I headed in that direction, wondering nervously just how far Phyllis was going to let me go before calling it off. At about 300 feet and somewhere around half a mile from where I planned my touchdown, I seriously doubted her judgment. I pulled on a notch of flaps and kept glancing back and forth at the pasture ahead and the altimeter.

"Okay," Phyllis said, "pull out."

I'm sure she heard my sigh of relief.

"That wasn't *bad*," she said. "But you'd have been better off circling more to the east and finding someplace in that flatter country over there."

Back up to 1000 feet, and *she did it again!* "Okay, now this time I want you to put it into a glide, find a good spot to land, set up a pattern and then go through your emergency checklist."

This time I picked a flat pasture and hurriedly went through the checklist—switch fuel tanks, turn on the electric fuel pump, give the engine a dose of carburetor heat . . .

"Better check which way the wind is blowing," Phyllis said calmly. Her tone sounded ludicrous in my state of mind.

"Out of the southwest," I said pointing to the ripples in a small pond below.

"Good. That means you're going to have a slight crosswind when you land."

Land? I banked into my final leg, and it looked to me as though we were awfully high for a touchdown in that pasture.

"Add some flaps—another notch," Phyllis ordered.

I complied. The Cherokee seemed to almost stop in the air and hold altitude.

"Okay, you're still high, drop the nose a little— watch that airspeed—and pull on full flaps."

By now I was convinced we were going to land in

that pasture—whether it was the original plan or not. Then I spotted the fence running right across the middle—perpendicular to our path and about a hundred yards beyond touchdown.

"Damn! A fence!" I muttered.

"Drop the nose some—you're losing airspeed. Good. Okay, pull out."

Whew!

"Not bad," Phyllis said. "We'd have made that."

"What about that fence, though?"

"It was little. Don't worry about those fences once you're on the ground. You can't always be *that* picky."

As we headed back to the airport, Phyllis discussed emergency procedures with me—something I'll go into later in the book.

"Now I want you to get some solo time practicing the maneuvers we've been working on the last few weeks," she said. "But not the emergency landings—you'll do some more of those later, but not by yourself."

"Don't worry!"

The next few times I went up by myself it was hard not to forget practicing and just fly around and enjoy the view. But I remembered Phyllis emphasizing the importance of polishing my skills and mastering the airplane before that flight test. Those S turns, and turns over a point, aren't just busy work—they teach you how to maneuver the airplane in reference to a ground point while correcting for drift, maintaining altitude and dividing your attention between flying and something on the ground.

Students often have trouble with this maneuver be-

Turns around a point demand top piloting skill—correcting for wind drift, maintaining altitude and dividing your attention between coordinating the controls and watching your target. Any stationary landmark can be used, but an intersection like this one is always the best choice.

cause they can't convince themselves that the steepest bank is necessary when the airplane is headed downwind, and the most shallow when it is moving into the wind. You have to correct for wind drift by adjusting the bank of the airplane at different positions during the turn. On the upwind side of the turn the wind will force you into making too narrow a turn if you don't level off your roll, while on the downwind swing the wind will carry you away from the point if you don't increase your bank. Another problem some students have is in picking the right reference point. Choose something like a barn, factory or the intersection of two roads or fences. You want something that's not going to move. That cluster of cows or tractor trailer stopped along the road may make interesting reference points—but it might get a little tough to maintain a constant radius if the cows start wandering around or the truck driver pulls away and heads off down the highway.

Using intersections is the best choice. If the wing blocks your vision (which it usually does at some point in the circle) you can still see the fence or road farther out and project it mentally to where the two lines intersect.

When you practice these maneuvers you'll be flying at a relatively low altitude (500 to 1000 feet), so find a place where there aren't a lot of people or livestock below. An airplane buzzing around and around continuously at that altitude can be pretty unnerving to folks and animals on the ground. And be sure the area offers a fairly safe place for an emergency landing in

Flying the hood. The hardest part is trusting the instruments and not your senses.

case something should go wrong. That low to the ground you won't be able to glide very far.

Similar considerations follow for making S turns across a road. The first step is to find a road running perpendicular to the wind direction. The objective is to fly two perfect half circles of equal size on opposite sides of the road. As with other ground-reference maneuvers, the practice altitude should be relatively low. As the road is crossed, the pilot should smoothly and gradually roll into a turn in the opposite direction. Just as in turns around a point, you must consider wind direction and velocity, and make corrections accordingly in order to avoid drifting off course.

The steepest angle of bank in a constant-radius turn is at the point of *greatest ground speed*. The steeper bank and higher rate of turn are required to turn the aircraft faster, since its speed over the ground has increased. This point of greatest ground speed is where the airplane is flying directly downwind—and the true airspeed plus the wind speed results in the higher ground speed. By contrast, the shallowest angle of bank is at the point of slowest ground speed. The shallower bank and slower rate of turn are necessary because the airplane is passing over the ground more slowly. This point of slowest ground speed occurs when the airplane is going directly into the wind. At this point, the true airspeed minus the wind speed results in the slower ground speed.

A lot of student pilots mistakenly think that the steepest and shallowest banks occur when the airplane is flying directly crosswind. But the airplane's ground speed remains the same, since the crosswind adds neither a headwind nor a tailwind to the ground speed. So, to make a turn that traces a perfect circle over the ground, the angle of bank must be changed constantly throughout the entire circular maneuver. The bank is gradually steepened from its shallowest point until the steepest bank is achieved when the airplane is flying directly downwind. And from the point where the airplane is flying directly downwind, the bank is gradually shallowed.

But there's more. While making constant-radius turns in a wind, the airplane must be flown with a *drift correction angle*, or crab. This means that on the downwind side of the turn, the nose must be crabbed *toward* the center of the circle. On the upwind side, it must be crabbed away from the circle's center.

It sounds easy, but when you're first learning, these maneuvers can foster some of a student pilot's most frustrating moments in an airplane. Next, I suppose, to landing.

Even without the added nuisance of wind drift, some of my S turns and circles wouldn't rate very high marks in penmanship or piloting either. So, each day I suppressed the urge to cruise along the lush valleys and ruggedly beautiful beaches of northern California, and methodically practiced, practiced and practiced those infernal turns until I thought I would get dizzy. I'd comb the area for different reference points (one of my favorites was the snack bar at a drive-in theater) and wonder when I was going to move on to bigger and better things.

Acceptable performance for ground-reference maneuvers is evaluated on the basis of planning, orientation, drift correction, altitude control and how well you can divide your attention among all these things. Even your airspeed shouldn't vary more than 10 mph. Admittedly, these maneuvers can become a little wearisome, but they're important to perfect. Sometimes, to break up the routine, I'd return to the airport for some touch-and-go landings, using normal flaps and sometimes adding a second notch or pulling on full flaps. This is good practice for what is called short-field takeoffs and landings. Not all airports (and other places you may want or have to land at) have long runways or plenty of clearance at either end.

During short-field practice sessions, it's always assumed that in addition to a short runway there are obstructions at each end of the runway that must be cleared. The takeoff checklist is the same as for any normal takeoff, except that you drop the flaps two notches (25 degrees) on the Piper Cherokee. (The recommended flap setting will vary with different airplanes.) Then, instead of easing on the throttle and beginning your takeoff run, you set the brakes and apply full power. The airplane will rock and sway under the power as the engine winds up to maximum rpm. When you release the brakes, the airplane seems like a dragster as it leaps forward and roars down the runway. Don't pull back on the control wheel until reaching a speed of 55 to 60 mph. Then apply only slight back pressure and you'll be airborne almost immediately. It's important not to raise the nose too soon, or you'll add too much drag and require longer take-off roll.

As the airplane climbs, pull back on the control wheel just enough to keep your speed at 78 to 80 mph, until you have cleared the obstacles. This speed (in the Piper Cherokee) is what's known as the *best angle-of-climb speed.* As soon as you've cleared the obstructions, release the flaps and ease the airplane into a more shallow climb attitude until reaching the *best rate-of-climb speed* of 90 mph. From there on out, the climb-out will be just like any other. It's important during these short-field takeoffs, however, to keep an eye on the airspeed indicator to avoid stalling—an adventure we'll go into shortly.

The successful short-field landing over an obstacle begins—as always—with good planning. To make the landing roll as short as possible, you want to touch down at minimum speed and as close to the obstacle as possible. This means clearing the obstruction by the least amount of distance at a high angle of descent and slow airspeed.

The early part of the approach on downwind leg and through the turn to base leg is very similar to a normal approach. During the latter part of the down-wind leg, some instructors prefer to extend the first notch, then the second notch on base, and full flaps on final approach while progressively reducing airspeed. This is to give you a feel for making a slower landing at roughly 75 mph, instead of the usual 90 mph. And the difference is tremendous! When you pull on that final notch of flaps it feels as though the airplane

Practicing slow flight is one of the ways a student pilot gains a feel for the airplane. In this photo the author is cruising along at only 60 mph with two notches of flaps at not quite 2100 rpm. The idea is to hold altitude. Notice the vertical speed indicator (under the altimeter) pegged right on zero. That's worth an "A" for the day!

literally is going to stop in midair and drop straight to the ground. And this is where you begin drawing on some earlier training—*power controls altitude; stabilator (or elevator) controls airspeed.* Keep your right hand locked on that throttle, and if you start dropping faster or sooner than desired—give it some power. Quickly. But not too much.

In slow flight, back pressure on the control wheel will raise the nose, slow the airspeed and increase the rate of descent. Altitude and angle of glide are controlled by power. Power is added to decrease the rate of descent and angle of glide. You'll want to hold that airplane up as long as necessary and then drop or glide down at a steep angle. It's a little unnerving the first couple of times you try it, and on my first full-flap landing attempt I glided nearly halfway down a 5000 foot runway before I finally settled the Cherokee down to earth again.

To steepen the glide angle, reduce power and maintain correct attitude and airspeed by working the stabilator. It isn't really difficult, but the radical angle of descent tends to spook most students a little the first couple of times. The main thing to remember is to keep adding power if necessary until you've cleared the obstacle (imaginary or not), and then cut the throttle and let the airplane settle down until time to pull back for flare-out right before touchdown.

A common problem for most students is finding themselves both *too low* and *too slow*. And the typical reaction seems to be to pull back on the controls to gain altitude. But that only slows you down more and increases the rate of descent. It's also hard for most students to adjust the nose downward, since it appears as if you're flying right into the ground. But that's what you should do—along with plenty of added power. You'll then maintain or even gain some altitude and pick up any speed necessary to extend the landing approach.

After clearing the obstacle, don't attempt to change the rate or angle of descent until time for flare-out. If you've done everything just right, you'll touch down very close to stalling speed. Pull back on the control wheel to keep the weight off the nose gear (assuming you're in a tri-gear airplane) and slowly, but firmly, apply the brakes.

As you grow skilled at short-field landings you'll be amazed at how little space is needed to set a small plane down. The trouble is, some pilots land in places they can't get out of. Better size things up well from the air before you get caught in that predicament. It might be kind of embarrassing if someday you had to call the place where you rented an airplane to tell them you need a tow truck because you landed in a picturesque little meadow for a picnic and there isn't enough room for takeoff. Go ahead and laugh—but it has happened.

And speaking of meadows—soft-field landings and takeoffs are another important dimension of pilot training. As a student you may not be required to actually land on a grass strip or the beach, but knowing how to handle these situations—for whatever reason they might occur—will make you a much better pilot.

Soft-field takeoffs begin much the same way as the short-field variety, or any other kind. Follow the checklist and normal run-up procedure, and then, just as in short-field takeoffs, drop two notches of flap. But instead of setting the brakes and running the engine up to full power, taxi slowly, without stopping, toward takeoff position to prevent the airplane from bogging down. Use full back pressure on the controls to keep weight off that front wheel.

As you taxi into position and line up for the takeoff, advance the throttle as rapidly as possible without causing the engine to falter. As speed picks up, you can relax some of the back pressure—but keep pulling just enough to hold most of the weight off that front wheel. The nose may be so high as you begin takeoff roll that you'll have to look more out of the side to see where you're going. Because of the angle of attack of the wings, you may lift off at a speed slower than the usual stalling speed. If so, relax the controls slightly once you gain a little altitude in order to pick up airspeed. Then gradually ease back on the wheel again to obtain your best angle-of-climb airspeed (about 78–80 mph) until you've cleared any obstacles and can level off into a more shallow or normal climb. Then retract the flaps.

Sometimes on rough surfaces the airplane will bounce or skip into the air before it actually reaches flying speed. When this happens (and a good pilot should be able to tell), don't change the angle of attack. If you pull back on the controls it may stall. On the other hand, the reverse reaction will hurtle the airplane back

Coming in for a full-flap landing. You've got to keep that nose pointed down or you're in for a stall.

to the ground right on the nosewheel, which will make it almost impossible to control and could very well result in a nasty flip called a ground loop. Either way, you may be facing a big repair bill.

One of the most unnerving maneuvers a student pilot must learn is the stall. It's something of a contradiction, I guess, that skilled pilots avoid stalls and students learn to perfect them.

Although students are required to practice stalls, the idea is not to be able to stall an airplane with perfection, but rather to learn how to recover quickly with a minimum loss of altitude. Modern airplanes are designed to recover from stalls without any assistance from the pilot. And in some cases, the pilot's interference only hinders recovery. But before we get into the aerodynamics of stalls, and how to pull out of them gracefully (and calmly), let's quickly review their cause.

Stalls are not the result of a lack of airspeed, but rather too great an angle of attack of the wings. The angle of attack is the angle between the wing-chord line and the direction that the wing is moving. Air moves toward the wing from the direction in which the wing is moving, or along the flight path of the airplane. In normal flight, air flows over the top of the wing and "hugs" it. But even at cruising speed, at a certain point back on the wing, the smooth air eventually tears away from the wing. This is called the *separation point*.

As the angle of attack increases, the separation point moves forward. Because of the angle of attack, it eventually reaches a point where too much air has separated from the wing and there is no longer enough lift to support the airplane. You then have a stall.

Student pilots are usually apprehensive about stalls out of fear the airplane will plunge to the ground, hopelessly out of control. And that strange sensation of feeling that your stomach is rushing up to meet your throat doesn't help either. But in reality, the only time a stall is risky is during the final stages of landing when both altitude and airspeed are lowest. Even then, a skilled and alert pilot can handle the situation without difficulty. It's because stalls are more apt to occur during this critical stage of flight that it's important for all pilots to know how to recover from them.

A student's first introduction to stalls usually begins from a power-off, wings-level glide similar to a landing approach. To enter the stall, the pilot will reduce power to idle, establish a normal glide and then gradually pull back on the controls to slow the airplane. It's a good learning experience to hesitate every time the airplane loses five miles an hour and move the aileron and rudder controls to get a feel for the airplane at slow speed. As speed drops, the response of the airplane to control pressure becomes slower or "mushy," as you'll hear around the hangar. These are all clues that the airplane is nearing a stall situation, and it's part of building your "seat-of-the-pants" feel for flying to learn this.

But there are plenty of other clues for the alert pilot. As the airplane approaches the stall, the student will get the feeling that the airplane is "mushing" or sinking. Stall warnings will begin 5 to 10 miles an hour before the stall. In the Cherokee the stall warning is a red light on the instrument panel in front of the pilot. In other airplanes it may be a buzzer, or something else. But whatever the stall warning, you'll know something is amiss. As the airplane continues to slow down, the engine will sound as if it's racing madly, while the outside wind noise virtually disappears.

It should be obvious by now that there is just no way you can stall an airplane unless you're dozing at the controls. But what usually happens is that a pilot, on a landing approach, gets busy with the myriad things to do on these final moments of flight, gets into a near stall situation—*and panics*. What does he do? He pulls back abruptly on the controls to hold altitude and—*voila!*—a complete stall.

The correct action, of course, should have been just the opposite. Dip the nose to gain airspeed and then feed the engine a little throttle if it's really necessary. But don't jam the control wheel forward, either. And that's why practicing stalls as a student is important. All moves have to be smooth and can't be overdone. Too much nose-down attitude will result in a loss of altitude—and on a landing approach that can be hazardous. Generally, all that's necessary to pull out of a stall is to relax pressure on the controls and let the airplane find its normal attitude.

After you gain a feel for stalls and get used to that weird sinking feeling that accompanies them, you should practice them as much as possible before taking your private-pilot flight test. What the examiner will be looking for is how well you recover, without losing more than 200 feet of altitude, and avoid a secondary stall. Secondary stalls are usually the result of a pilot recovering from the first stall, then pulling back on the controls too soon and winding up in another one. It takes some practice, but you'll gain a tremendous feel for the airplane. And be sure you do your stalls at 2000 feet or more to give yourself a wide margin for error.

After a few hours of practicing these maneuvers you will have picked up a good feel for the airplane and gained that all-important self-confidence. You'll feel comfortable flying and enjoy it more—but don't get cocky. Carelessness is what gets even the most experienced pilots in trouble. The good pilot is one who realizes that flying is a continuous learning process— you *never* know it all. And that's part of the fun.

6
Highways
in
the
Sky

As you might have already guessed, learning to fly the airplane is only part of flight training. The real fun— and work—begins after you've mastered most of the basics. Then it's time to learn how to travel from here to there without getting lost.

It was when I first began studying navigation that I realized that flying is part art and part science. The art lies in developing your skills at learning to fly the airplane—making smooth takeoffs, coordinated turns and graceful landings. Science enters the picture in the form of navigation and meteorology. And no matter how good you may become at flying the airplane, you'll never take that step up to being a pilot until you understand weather and can navigate. After all, no matter how sharp you are at making turns around a point, S turns over a road and then returning to Mother Earth in one piece, flying involves more than wandering a few miles from home base and practicing maneuvers. You want to *go* somewhere, right?

But there are no signposts in the sky that tell you to turn right or left at the next intersection. Flying an airplane requires much more awareness. At the same time, it permits you considerably more freedom than the frustrated motorist caught in the maze of congested freeways and city streets. And the view is much better. But while the idea of navigation may initially seem frightening, as you progress in cross-country training (which constitutes most of your flight training after your solo experience) you will soon discover a new sense of accomplishment and independence. But it *does* take some practice. And it's not always easy, because the land below often bears even less resemblance to the map in your lap than a policeman's composite drawing of a suspect does to the real criminal's face. So, navigating demands more than merely comparing the ground with the map and checking off your progress.

Sunlight does strange things to the shapes of mountains and valleys. Roads that stand out on maps dissolve into a blur of colors; angles and heights become nearly impossible to judge without lengthy experience; and the distances of objects on the horizon vary in proportion to the amount of air pollution between you and them.

But like most things foreign, navigation sounds more difficult to the beginner than it really is. Basically, it requires an alert person who pays attention to where he's going and keeps track of where he's been. The ideal pilot in the absurdly unrealistic written test for private pilots is a compulsive sort who methodically calculates before the flight the distance from checkpoint to checkpoint and the predicted times and headings between them, and then keeps up this tiresome book-keeping throughout the entire flight by filling in the times and headings flown. While you are learning to fly, your instructor will make you go through all these tedious measures—and like military service, it's probably good training of some sort. But if you really did all that on every trip, flying would be about as much fun as basic training. So don't let the rigors of navigation training turn you off to the joy of flying. You'll catch on pretty quickly after a couple of cross-country efforts.

There are several types of navigation used by pilots: (1) *pilotage*, or flying by reference to landmarks; (2) *dead (deduced) reckoning*, which is drawing vectors of the wind and your true airspeed and computing the heading, ground speed and estimated time of arrival at the destination; and (3) *radio navigation*, or navigation through the use of radio aids.

Pilotage is the most common method used by most students and private pilots, although the use of radio is growing as light airplanes become better equipped. Pilotage is simply proceeding from one checkpoint to another, keeping them close enough together to make it impossible to drift out of sight of the course on the way from one to the next. The experienced and careful pilot (and I've met very few experienced ones who *weren't* careful) remembers where he has been and looks ahead to where he is going. He has always identified many more—and more remote—landmarks on the chart than he actually needs in order to find his way. Keep track of where you are and what the surrounding terrain looks like. Know in advance what you are looking for, and not only look for major landmarks, but compare everything you see with the chart—not consciously and exhaustively, but in a relaxed and routine fashion.

The alert pilot becomes, without meaning to, a good amateur geologist and geographer, and he learns to visualize the terrain from the contour lines on the chart before he ever arrives there. In the back of your mind, keep track of the valleys and roads, including the ones that may be out of sight behind hills to either side of your course. If you ever have engine trouble or some other kind of emergency, you don't want to waste time scrambling around with a stack of maps trying to find the best place to set her down!

Keep track of which way the wind is blowing and roughly how fast, in relation to your own heading. You can pick up a great deal of helpful information about the wind by observing cloud shadows, which way smoke travels after it leaves smokestacks, water ripples on lakes and how the airplane climbs or descends as it crosses ridges. In mountainous states you can identify distant peaks and hold a heading on them rather than

Filing a flight plan isn't required by the FAA, but it's a good practice for your own safety.

on the sometimes elusive numbers of the compass window. In the Midwest you can focus on other landmarks such as shapes of towns, rivers and railroads.

In desolate areas like the desert, or at night, the modern pilot can usually rely on radio navigation if his plane is so equipped. And most of them are today. In fact, modern radio aids have so altered aerial navigation that navigation has ceased to be one of the pilot's major concerns. With a basic autopilot costing less than $1000, a pilot can remain almost totally ignorant of his position throughout most of the flight and still arrive on target and on time by checking in periodically along the way and making any necessary corrections. It isn't

PILOT'S PREFLIGHT CHECK LIST

DATE 6-20-74

✓ WEATHER ADVISORIES	ALTERNATE WEATHER	NOTAMS
✓ EN ROUTE WEATHER	FORECASTS	AIRSPACE RESTRICTIONS
✓ DESTINATION WEATHER	✓ WINDS ALOFT	MAPS

FLIGHT LOG

DEPARTURE POINT	VOR IDENT.	RADIAL TO	DISTANCE / LEG	TIME PT-TO-PT CUMULATIVE	TAKEOFF	GROUND SPEED
STS	FREQ.	FROM	REMAINING			
CHECK POINT CALISTOGA	STS 104.9	39°	12.5 65.5	12.5	ETA 0946 ATA 0946	90
GUINDA	MYU 110.8	"	27 38.5	27	1000 1002	108
DUNNIGAN	110.8	"	12 26.5		1009 1009	108
GRIMES	110.8	"	12 14.5		1016 1015	111
MYU			14.5 —		1023 1023	111
DESTINATION MYU		TOTAL	78			

POSITION REPORT: FVFR report hourly, IFR as required by ATC

ACFT. IDENT.	POSITION	TIME	ALT.	IFR/VFR	EST. NEXT FIX	NAME OF SUCCEEDING FIX	PIREPS

REPORT CONDITIONS ALOFT— CLOUD TOPS, BASES, LAYERS, VISIBILITY, TURBULENCE, HAZE, ICE, THUNDERSTORMS

CLOSE FLIGHT PLAN UPON ARRIVAL

The cross-country navigation log can be a lifesaver if you get lost.

recommended practice, but it is commonplace, none-theless.

But whatever methods of navigation you choose to use for a particular trip, success begins on the ground with thorough planning. When preparing for a cross-

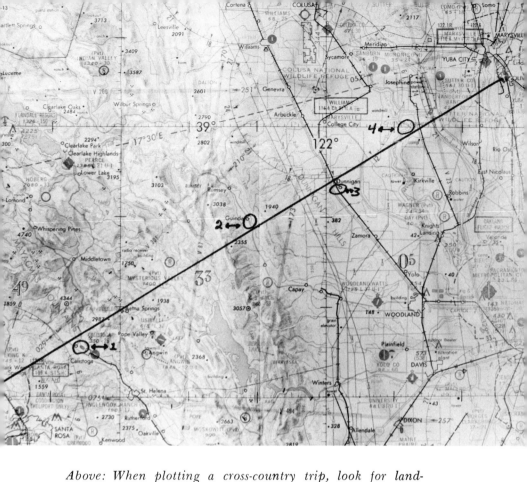

Above: When plotting a cross-country trip, look for landmarks that will make distinctive checkpoints. See aerial photos. Below: Right on schedule over the first checkpoint—the half-mile dirt oval speedway at Calistoga.

Above: Checkpoint 2, a creek. Below: Checkpoint 3. There are the highway and the railroad tracks.

Above: Checkpoint 4. That distinctive horseshoe shape made this small river a good checkpoint. Below: There's Marysville! Right on time. Sometimes airports are difficult for student pilots to see from a distance, but you learn in time.

country flight, a pilot should have navigation charts for the intended route, a plotter, computer, flight-planning sheets and access to the *Airman's Information Manual*. Federal Aviation Regulation (FAR) Part 91.5 states that each pilot in command shall, before beginning a flight, familiarize himself with all available information concerning that flight. This information must include, for a flight not in the vicinity of an airport, available weather reports and forecasts, fuel availability and consumption, runway requirements, pilot qualifications and alternatives available if the planned flight cannot be completed. While filing a flight plan is not required by the FARs, it's still good operating practice, since it aids in search and rescue—and improves your chances many times over of being located in case of a forced landing or other such emergency.

The place where every cross-country flight should begin is at a table or desk with a sectional chart, a computer, plotter and a felt-tip pen. Sectional charts are the charts most commonly used by private pilots. Each sectional chart shows a portion of the United States and is identified by the name of a principal city, such as San Francisco, Dallas–Fort Worth or New York. The scale on the sectional chart is 1:500,000 or about eight miles to one inch.

The sectional chart contains topographical information which features a portrayal of the terrain relief and also includes visual checkpoints such as cities, towns, villages, lakes, rivers, drainages, roads, railroads and other distinctive landmarks used in VFR (visual flight rules) flight. Aeronautical information on the sectional

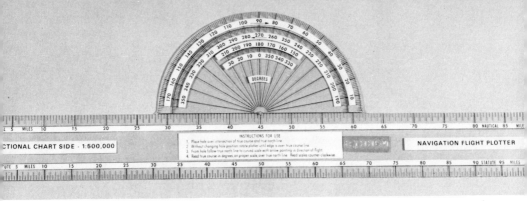

This handy plastic plotter is used for drawing cross-country courses, measuring mileage and figuring magnetic heading. The reverse side is the same except it's used for WAC charts.

chart includes visual and radio aids to navigation, airports, controlled airspace, special use airspace, obstructions and related information. Sectional charts are revised and issued every six months.

World Aeronautical Charts (WAC) are similar to sectional charts except that WAC charts are drawn to a scale one half that of the sectional. WAC charts use a 1:1,000,000 scale, which is about 16 miles to one inch, and, therefore, omit some of the detail found on the sectionals. WAC charts are usually used for navigation of higher performance airplanes or for long trips where frequent change of charts en route would be a nuisance. Each WAC is identified by a number. WAC charts are revised and issued once a year.

The plotter is a small, transparent plastic circle or semicircle marked from zero to 360 degrees (the semicircular plotter has a double row of figures at each point) to measure course angles on the map. Plotters have an attached plastic rule in scale miles for both the sectional and WAC charts. When you plan a cross-country flight, you'll draw a line (or lines) between your departure airport and the destination airport and measure the true course with the plotter.

A computer is a useful addition to any pilot's equipment. It's a circular slide rule with the inside circle calibrated in time (hours and minutes) and the outside circle in velocity (miles per hour or knots) or gallons. With it you can check fuel consumption or speed. On the reverse side of most computers you can figure wind correction or drift. Computers are easy to operate and a lifesaver for those of us who don't have a gift for mathematics.

When plotting the course, a straight line should be drawn from the center of the departure airport to the center of the first point where a direction change is made. The pilot should examine his route closely to ensure compliance with airspace restrictions. Terrain elevation along the route should be determined to assure adherence to proper VFR altitudes. All aircraft flying more than 3000 feet above ground level (AGL) are supposed to fly at odd thousands plus 500 feet when traveling on a magnetic course of zero through 179 degrees, and even thousands plus 500 feet when flying magnetic courses between 180 and 360 degrees. Consideration must also be given to the performance of the airplane when picking your cruising altitude, since most airplanes have an optimum cruise altitude. You can find this in the owner's handbook.

When reviewing the cross-country flight, the pilot must make sure the airplane is within its legal weight and balance limits, according to the owner's handbook. You should not only consider weight, but also load distribution. If passengers, cargo or fuel are not all in their respective positions and within CG (center of gravity) limits, the airplane will be off balance, reducing stability, control response and performance. This is where too many private pilots are negligent, and improper loading is responsible for a large share of takeoff crashes.

After the true course has been drawn, prominent

Left: This multipurpose hand computer is a convenient aid in cross-country navigation.
Right: On the wind side of the computer you can figure how winds aloft will cause you to drift and make the necessary corrections in your magnetic heading.

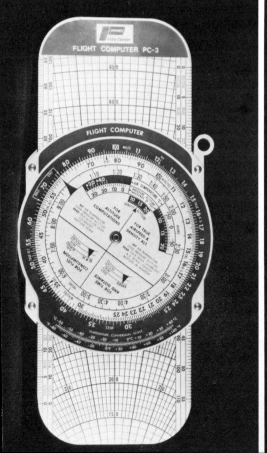
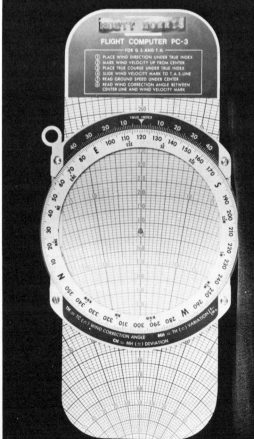

checkpoints are selected along the route and circled with a color that can be seen easily. These checkpoints will be needed during the flight to verify positions and to make checks on the ground speed. This is what's known as dead reckoning navigation. Once the checkpoints are selected, they are recorded in a navigation log so that they can be referred to during the flight. The next step in planning is the measurement of distances using the navigation plotter (see photo on page 143), then entering the distances between each checkpoint and the total distance in the log. Using the flight computer, the pilot will then compute how long it will take to fly from checkpoint to checkpoint, figuring average airspeed. The navigation log will have a column for writing in the estimated time of arrival at each checkpoint, and another column for the actual time of arrival at that checkpoint.

The next items to be determined are the magnetic courses. Actually, magnetic courses are nothing more than true courses corrected for *magnetic variation*. There's an old saying in flying circles that *east is least and west is best*. This has absolutely nothing to do with geographic preference. It means that east variation is subtracted and west variation is added to the true course to obtain the magnetic course. The fact that the magnetic north pole and the true north pole are not the same means a little more work for you in navigating. The magnetic north pole is in Canada, and your compass points to this magnetic pole rather than the true one. The angle between your direction to *true north* and *magnetic north* is called variation. The vari-

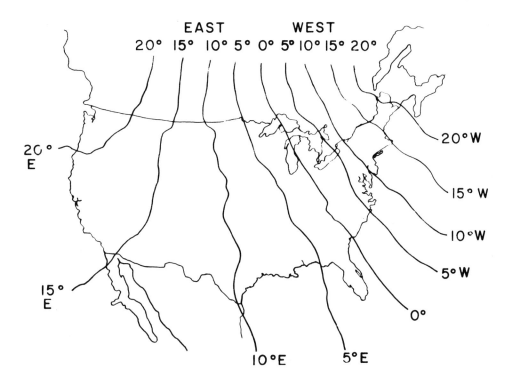

Approximate location of isogonic lines in the United States.

ation in the United States runs from about 22 degrees west in Maine to about 20 degrees east in Oregon.

Isogonic lines, or lines of equal variation, appear on the aeronautical charts and are given in one-degree increments. If you should be flying in an area where the two poles are in line, no correction for variation is necessary. The isogonic line will show as zero degrees variation, or more properly, the zero-degree line is called the *agonic line.* In the United States, the agonic line runs roughly through Lake Michigan southeast into the Atlantic Ocean just east of Florida. Any pilot east of that line would add the magnetic variation number to his true course heading, while pilots flying west of that divider would subtract. For example, if you measured the true course with a plotter and found it to be 120 degrees, and the midpoint isogonic line showed 5 degrees east, your magnetic heading would then be 115 degrees.

The terms *east* and *west* used for variation may be misleading or confusing for the newcomer. They might appear to have something to do with the direction the airplane is flying. *This is not the case at all.* It refers to your relationship to the agonic line. And to add to the confusion, if you're east of that divider, the isogonic lines are in degrees west, while the reverse is true for those of us residing west of the zero-degree variation marker. It would probably be a lot clearer to speak in terms of "plus 5 degrees variation" or "minus 5 degrees variation," but every activity and profession seems to have its own special jargon, and the current method appears to be permanent.

All compasses suffer from an ailment known as *deviation,* due in part from attraction by the ferrous metal

All compasses suffer from an ailment known as deviation, due in part to attraction by the ferrous metal parts of the airplane. This error will vary between headings and is usually noted for every 30 degrees on a compass correction card, located on the instrument panel near the compass.

parts of the airplane. This error will vary between headings, and is usually noted for every 30 degrees on a compass correction card, which is located on the instrument panel near the compass. The compass is swung or corrected on a compass rose, a large calibrated circle painted on the concrete ramp or taxiway away from metal interference such as hangars. The airplane is taxied onto the rose, and corrections are made with a nonmagnetic screwdriver.

For the steps used to go from a true course (or true heading) to the course (or heading) with respect to the compass, remember that "*T*rue *V*irgins *M*ake *D*ull *C*ompany":

1. *True* course (or heading)
2. Plus or minus *Variation* gives
3. *Magnetic* course (or heading)
4. Plus or minus *Deviation* gives
5. *Compass* course (or heading).

Remember that the "east is least . . ." idea is true only when going from a true course (or heading) to a magnetic course or heading. Working from magnetic to true, you would *add* easterly variation and *subtract* westerly variation. The normal procedure is to go from true to magnetic courses or headings, but written tests have asked questions on the reverse procedure. So be on the alert!

After you have plotted your course, figured the magnetic heading to follow and know how long the trip will take, the next step is to find out how much fuel the airplane will use during the trip. Fuel-consumption rate can be found in the owner's handbook, and the computer can be used to figure how much you'll burn on the trip. If you're going to have to stop somewhere along the line for refueling, make sure you plan a stop long before your supply runs low. That way, in case you hit a headwind or happen to drift off course, you won't chance running out of gas.

Dead-reckoning navigation and pilotage are very similar, except that the former, as the name implies, is much more exacting, and much harder. But in recent years, advances in radio equipment have made navigation far more exacting, safer and almost effortless.

Radio navigation stations consist of two basic types: VOR (very high frequency omnidirectional range) and Nondirectional Radio Beacons. Each of these radio facilities performs different functions that can be used individually or collectively by the pilot for navigating with varying weather, altitude and terrain conditions. In addition to the basic radio navigation systems, other electronic equipment, such as DME (distance-measuring equipment) and transponders are available to ease the pilot's workload.

Knowing how to use the various facilities provided by the FAA for air traffic control is one of the most important areas of aeronautical knowledge. The air traffic control (ATC) system is based on voice communications between ATC controllers and pilots, requiring an expansive network of communication facilities. These facilities can be divided into terminal and en-route services, both of which are important for providing traffic separation and weather information.

Radio frequencies are identified by numerical values, depending upon the number of cycles per second (hertz) made by the specific frequency. Due to the very high number of cycles involved, it's convenient to use the terms *kilohertz* (kHz) and *megahertz* (MHz) when referring to frequencies. One thousand cycles per second equals one kilohertz and one million cycles per second denotes one megahertz.

A radio frequency band refers to a group of frequencies with an upper and lower cycle limit. There are four frequency bands which are used in aviation communications. They are: L/MF (low/medium frequency range), HF (high frequency range), VHF (very high frequency range) and UHF (ultrahigh frequency

VOR radio navigation equipment has taken most of the work (and fun, some think) out of navigating.

range). The low frequency range is from 30 to 300 kHz, and the medium frequency range extends from 300 to 3000 kHz. Lower frequencies allocated by the Federal Communications Commission for aircraft communications extend from 200 to 415 kHz, including portions of both the low and medium frequency range. This aircraft band is referred to as the L/MF band.

The HF band includes frequencies from 3000 to 30,000 kHz. Although many frequencies in this range have been allocated to aviation, the use of high frequencies has gradually decreased to the point that the high frequency band is no longer considered an important system of communications for domestic operations. The very high frequency (VHF) band is the most important portion of the frequency spectrum to the private pilot and includes frequencies from 30 MHz to 300 MHz.

The frequency range of 108.00 MHz through 117.95 MHz is used for air navigation aids, such as instrument landing systems (ILS) and VOR, and provides simultaneous voice reception over these frequencies. The frequency range allotted for civil aviation voice communication is from 118.00 MHz to 135.95 MHz. It should be emphasized that the VHF band is by far the most commonly used in general aviation. The UHF band includes frequencies from 300 MHz to 3000 MHz. This band of frequencies has been reserved for use by various government agencies including the military. In addition, distance-measuring equipment and the glide slope (vertical guidance) portion of the ILS system operate with signals in the UHF band.

The low/medium and high frequencies can be bounced back from the ionosphere (a shell of electrically charged particles surrounding the earth) and are not affected by intermediate obstruction or line-of-sight restrictions. These frequencies are helpful to the pilot for low altitude, long-range reception of navigational signals and weather information. The greatest disadvantage is static, especially in stormy weather or rain. The biggest disadvantage of VHF and UHF frequencies is the line-of-sight limitation. Any obstruction, including the earth's curvature, will interfere with VHF communications. The line-of-sight factor restricts the reception distance of VHF and UHF signals for low-altitude communications and navigation. In other words, the higher the aircraft, the better the reception.

Examples of various reception distances for VHF frequencies are listed below:

Feet above ground	Reception distance (nautical miles)
1000	39
3000	69
5000	87
10,000	122
15,000	152
20,000	174

One of the most valuable services available to pilots today is Automatic Terminal Information Service, which is recorded information provided at many major

The standard international VHF frequency is 121.5 MHz. Pilots flying airplanes equipped with radar transponders can dial in the emergency frequency of 7700, which will automatically alert radar stations.

air terminals to give the arriving and departing pilots advance information on active runways, weather conditions, communication frequencies and any NOTAMs affecting the airport at a particular time. ATIS has reduced ATC controller workloads by making it unnecessary for controllers to continually relay routine information. Instead, this information is recorded on a tape and transmitted continuously over an ILS, VOR or other commonly used frequency in the airport area. As airport conditions change—such as wind direction or velocity, altimeter setting or active runway—a new tape is made to reflect the new conditions. Each ATIS recording is coded with a phonetic letter of the alphabet, such as *information Alpha* or *information Echo*, and the pilot, on calling the tower, ground control or approach control, should state that he has received the current information:

Following is an example of a typical ATIS broadcast:

> This is Stapleton International Airport Information Quebec. Denver weather: measured ceiling five thousand overcast, visibility five miles in smoke and haze. Wind two five zero degrees at six, altimeter two niner eight seven. ILS runway two six left approaches in use. Landing runway two six left for large aircraft; runway two six right for light aircraft. Tower frequency one one eight point three. Departures are on runway three five, tower frequency one one niner point five. Advise Denver Tower, Approach Control or Ground Control on initial contact that you have received Information Quebec.

ATIS frequencies for airports incorporating the system can be found in the Airport/Facility Directory in Part 3 of AIM. On sectional charts, the ATIS frequency is included with other airport data.

Another major communications facility which the VFR pilot uses extensively is the flight service station (FSS). Flight service station attendants provide pilots with all types of flight information such as current altimeter settings, advisories on en route weather and any other information which would be of help on a cross-country flight. Flight service stations also can supply complete preflight weather briefings. The standard FSS communication frequencies and the codes used to indicate the available frequencies are listed in the "Radio Aids to Navigation" legend on the front panel of each sectional chart. One common method used in contacting flight service stations is to transmit on 122.1 MHz and receive the FSS on the VOR frequency. A standard frequency which may be used is 122.6 MHz. When using this frequency, it's possible to transmit and receive the flight service station on the same frequency. Another frequency common to flight service stations is 123.6 MHz.

When arriving at a non-tower-equipped airport where a flight service station is located, it's possible for the pilot to receive airport advisory service on the

A major communications facility which the VFR pilot uses extensively is the flight service station (FSS). Flight service station attendants provide pilots with all types of flight information such as current altimeter settings, advisories on en route weather and any other information which would be of help on a cross-country flight. They also can provide preflight weather briefings.

standard 123.6. Flight service stations exercise no control over arriving or departing traffic, but they can provide information on windspeed, direction, weather conditions and any known traffic in the area. It's always a good idea for a pilot arriving at an airport with FSS facilities to contact the station and request an airport advisory.

There are two VHF frequencies that seem to belong solely to general aviation. These are 122.8 and 123.0, which are privately operated radio stations and are known as UNICOM. The frequency of 122.8 MHz is used at many airports but is assigned only to those airports *not equipped* with control towers or flight service stations. At airports served by control towers or FSS, the frequency of 123.0 MHz is used in place of 122.8 for UNICOM.

The 122.8 frequency is often used to provide pilots with an airport advisory of wind directions and velocities, runway in use and any known traffic in the airport traffic pattern. You may also use this frequency to inquire about ground transportation, aircraft service and even eating facilities.

One of the frequencies all pilots should memorize is 121.5 MHz. This is the international frequency for emergency use. Flight service stations, control towers and air-route traffic-control centers maintain a listening watch on this single-channel communications frequency. The initial call should be "Mayday, Mayday, Mayday" if the pilot has an emergency or is in distress. If you're not in immediate distress but are uncertain of your situation and want to alert ground personnel, then your message should be prefaced with "pan, pan, pan."

For aircraft equipped with a radar beacon transponder, the emergency transponder code is 7700. If a pilot in a transponder-equipped aircraft experiences an emergency, he should select code 7700. Doing this will automatically activate an alarm at the appropriate radar facility. In addition, the radar blip of the aircraft will light up to a higher intensity on the radar screen.

Another aid to lost or disoriented pilots is D/F, or *direction-finding equipment*. The equipment consists of a directional antenna system and a radio receiver (both VHF and UHF). The D/F display indicates the magnetic direction of the aircraft from the station each time the airplane transmits. Where D/F equipment is tied into radar, a strobe of light is flashed from the center of the radar scope in the direction of the transmitting aircraft. In order to utilize D/F equipment, the pilot should contact the nearest D/F-equipped tower or flight service station on the VHF radio. Periodically, he will be requested to transmit, and after each transmission, personnel at the D/F station will give him an adjusted heading to fly to the station.

If an emergency or alert situation develops, the pilot should remember the four Cs:

1. *Confess* your predicament to any ground radio station. Don't wait too long.
2. *Communicate* with your ground radio link and pass on as much of the distress or alert message on the first transmission as possible.
3. *Climb*, if possible, for better radar and D/F

detection. If flying at low altitude, the pilot's chance for establishing radio contact is improved by climbing.

4. *Comply* with the advice and instructions received.

Any time a pilot is in doubt about his position or feels apprehensive for his safety, he should never hesitate to request assistance. Some of the finest and most experienced pilots around have been lost or confused at one time or another. Don't let foolish pride short-circuit your better judgment. Search and rescue facilities, including radar, radio and D/F stations, are ready and willing to help, and there is no penalty for using them. We'll go into considerably more detail on emergency procedures and forced landings in Chapter 10.

Emergency locator transmitters are required by law for all new aircraft delivered after January 1, 1972, and are valuable equipment for pilots flying over mountainous or sparsely populated terrain. Piper installs a unit called the Piper Automatic Locator (PAL) inside the fuselage near the base of the vertical fin. A longitudinal deceleration of five g's is normally required to activate this transmitter, or it can be turned on manually. Once activated, PAL sends out signals which, when picked up by appropriately equipped search aircraft, will lead searchers directly to a downed airplane or help them locate one by flying a search pattern.

In the early days of aviation, it became apparent that some sort of navigation system was necessary to assist pilots on cross-country trips, especially if the airplane was going to be useful as a transportation tool. One of the first such navigational aids were bonfires built by farmers and ranchers at predetermined times and locations. Obviously, with today's high-flying, super-fast airplanes cruising the airways, such a system would be worthless.

As technology advanced, a cross-country network of light beacons and emergency airfields assisted pilots. In 1926, these light beacons covered approximately 2000 miles; by 1929, more than 10,000 miles. But this system had its disadvantages, too. It was only effective at night and only when visibility was good.

Early in 1925, experimental work was begun utilizing a radio beacon which would produce a radio beam for navigational purposes. When put into use, these became known as radio range stations, and some are still in use in Alaska, Canada, Mexico and many other countries. The old radio range stations, however, were destined to give way to the new, more sophisticated VHF omnidirectional range system, which is the primary mode of navigation in the United States today. But automatic direction-finding equipment (ADF) is still a very important and integral part of modern radio navigation. Not only does it provide assistance in flying the old low/medium frequency range, but it also allows navigation to or from any nondirectional low- or medium-frequency radio station. ADF is used with nondirectional radio beacons, compass locators for the instrument-landing systems and standard (AM) broadcast stations.

The ADF receiver has a frequency selector or tuner, a volume control and a function switch similar to those of many personal radios used in the home. This type of radio requires careful tuning to select the correct station. Also available, as an option on most airplanes, is an ADF receiver with digital tuning, which provides a convenient means of positive station tuning. The receiver and bearing indicator give the pilot necessary navigational information. The bearing indicator has a 360-degree azimuth ring and a needle. On most ADF indicators, the azimuth is fixed, and zero represents the nose of the airplane.

When a station is tuned and the function selector knob is set to the ADF position, the needle on the indicator will point to the station, and a bearing relative to the nose of the airplane can be noted. If the magnetic heading of the airplane and the relative bearing on the ADF indicator are added together, you can determine the magnetic bearing to the station.

Through a procedure known as *tracking*, the airplane may be flown to or away from a radio station on any desired course. This method involves trial and error in determining the wind-correction angle. Another method of navigating with ADF is known as *homing*. This procedure is simple in that all the pilot has to do is continually change his heading so that the ADF indicator remains on zero. If there is a crosswind, however, the airplane will actually drift slightly downwind from the station rather than flying a direct course.

In the late 1940s, a very high frequency, omnidirectional range system of navigation was developed. Approximately 400 VOR stations had been installed by 1953 as VOR began to take the place of the low-frequency airway system. By mid 1972, there were almost 1000 VOR stations in the United States operated by the FAA, state agencies and private operators. Each VOR station transmits beams, called radials, outward in every direction. The VOR receiver on an airplane detects these signals and then indicates on which radial an aircraft is flying, thus enabling the pilot to follow a radial to or from a particular VOR. Each radial is numbered according to its *bearing* from the station. A compass rose is drawn around each VOR on a chart, with the 0-degree radial pointing toward magnetic north.

VOR is the most popular and easiest to use of all the various navigational aids. On a sectional or world aeronautical chart, a VOR-station symbol is shown in blue and is surrounded by an azimuth symbol. The calibrated azimuth surrounding the station is a built-in protractor corrected for local magnetic variation. Therefore, all you need to plot a course is something to draw a straight line with. Once airborne, the pilot turns the azimuth to the heading he wants, tunes in the correct frequency, turns the course selector until it reads either "to" or "from" and follows the needle in the center of the VOR dial. The idea is to *keep* the needle centered. When it's centered, you're on course. If it drifts to the left or right, you must fly in that direction to get back on course. VOR also eliminates a lot of work, since it automatically compensates for any wind drift. When flying *away* from an airport with a

VOR you might tune in the frequency for that VOR, and set the course selector on "from," until you are within range of the next station along your route.

Since VOR equipment is VHF, it's subject to line-of-sight restriction. There is some "spillover," however, and reception at an altitude of 1000 feet above the ground can be expected to be about 40 to 45 miles. This distance will increase with altitude.

Before following a VOR radial, however, a pilot should make sure he has the right station. There is only one positive method of indentifying a station—by listening to the Morse code identification or the recorded automatic voice identification. Automatic voice identification has been added to most VOR stations. When used, it's always indicated by the letters *VOR* following the station name, such as "Denver VOR," alternating with the usual Morse code identification. The Morse code identification and frequency are printed on the sectional and WAC charts.

Another radio that is commonly used in today's aircraft is *distance-measuring equipment*. DME consists of ground equipment installed in a VORTAC (co-located VOR and TACAN) station and equipment installed in the airplane. TACAN, which stands for tactical air navigation, is a military navigational aid. However, civil aviation can and does use a portion of the TACAN system for DME.

When in use, the airborne equipment sends out a signal which is picked up by the ground equipment. The ground equipment automatically returns a response to the airplane. DME in the airplane measures the elapsed time between the transmission of the original signal and the time that the response is received from the ground station. This information is then converted into an instrument indication that tells the pilot the *distance* from the station in *nautical miles.* If necessary, the pilot can then convert the nautical mileage into statute miles with his computer. DME, in addition to being useful for en route navigation, is also helpful in finding an airport, since it indicates the exact mileage from a VORTAC station.

With all the sophisticated radio equipment now available, no pilot today really has to be expert at pilotage. But even radio equipment has its limitations, and the wise pilot will employ more than one method of navigation while on a cross-country flight. And even though visual point-to-point navigation may seem primitive, it often has advantages over its electronic counterpart. While homing in on a VOR beam or radial is much simpler than plotting a course and watching for checkpoints, the "old-fashioned" pilotage method may offer a much more direct route. Most pilots will use VOR as a convenience, but it isn't always practical to plot a course from one VOR to another that may well take you twice as long to reach your destination and consume much more of that expensive fuel!

When selecting navigation checkpoints, pick landmarks that are clearly distinctive. But regardless of experience, anyone can get lost. If that ever happens, don't panic. The first step to follow is to stay on the original heading and watch for recognizable landmarks.

It's easy to miss a checkpoint because you flew directly over it or perhaps arrived a minute or two sooner than expected. This is where good pilotage and that bothersome navigation log can save the day. If you checked off your last position, know how long it's been since the last checkpoint and have been figuring your average ground speed, you shouldn't have trouble locating your position. Estimate the distance you've traveled since the last known checkpoint and, using this distance as a radius, draw a semicircle from that checkpoint on your sectional chart. Since it's fairly safe to assume you haven't made a 180-degree turn, your position should be somewhere within that semicircle. Scan the chart carefully for landmarks—chances are good to excellent that you have merely drifted a couple of miles or so downwind of your plotted course.

Although sectional charts are issued every six months, changes can still take place that might fool or confuse a pilot. Rivers may shrink or dry up altogether during the summer, towns grow, and new roads are built. Make sure your chart is the latest edition and then try to pick checkpoints that aren't likely to have changed considerably or vanished altogether in the past few weeks or months.

7
Flying
after
Dark

In many respects, flying at night is easier and more pleasant than flying during daylight hours. Traffic is usually easier to spot at night, and the air is generally smoother and cooler, resulting in more comfortable flight and better airplane performance. There is usually much less traffic around airports and considerably less verbal congestion on the radio.

But despite the advantages, you may face your first session of night flying with some trepidation. After you've been up a couple of times at night, however, you'll find that night flying expands both your piloting skills and self-confidence.

Most of all, however, it's just a lot of fun. This is especially true on a smooth, clear night when the pilot can turn the cabin lights down, relax and be drawn closer to the magic and mystery of flying as he watches the airplane's wings slide across the sparkling lights of a city, or traces automobile headlights strung along some highway like a rope of glittering beads.

You'll receive dual night-flying instruction before being turned loose on your own. The instructor will probably have you fly first around the local area at a good altitude to get you accustomed to night flying before bringing you back into the pattern for dual takeoffs and landings. It's during night flight that you'll really appreciate your training and experience under the hood. That horizon you unconsciously relied on for orientation during daylight flight vanishes at night. You'll find yourself having to rely more on the instruments—particularly the attitude indicator (artificial horizon), altimeter and airspeed indicator—than on your visual reference.

Our eyes and other senses also can play tricks on us or give us misleading information while flying at night. The results of this misinformation are manifest in illusions we must be alert to. A common illusion that many student pilots experience is feeling as though they're moving faster than they really are during the takeoff roll. This is caused by seeing the *nearby* objects, such as boundary lights on the runway, more clearly. They appear to move past the airplane in a rapid blur. Another common disorientation is that a normal landing approach looks steeper at night, creating an illusion of overshooting, which may actually result in landing short. This sensory disorientation is thought to be the reason so many pilots make lower approaches at night, even though they believe they are on a normal approach attitude.

The remedy for such illusions is mostly to pay careful attention to flying a normal traffic pattern and to use aids such as VASI (visual approach slope indicator) lights where they are available. VASI lights are a system of red and white lights which permit pilots to set up a correct landing approach by forming a sort of visual aiming point. The most common VASI arrangement is two rows of lights on either side of the runway. The first set, or row, is called the *downwind* row and is located about 600 feet beyond the runway threshold. The second row is referred to as the *upwind* set and is placed about 1300 feet from the threshold. Each VASI light box has a filter that splits the light beams into a white segment above a certain angle and a red segment below this angle. If a pilot is approaching a runway too high, the light beam appears white. On the other hand, if the approach is too low he sees a red beam. Since the objective is to land between the upwind row and the downwind row, the upwind row of lights should appear red and the downwind row look white to a pilot on a correct approach attitude or profile. Just remember, the proper light combination is *red over white.*

A safe and enjoyable night flight always begins with good thought and preparation on the ground. The preflight inspection should be made in the usual man-

VASI LIGHT UNIT

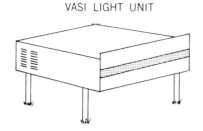

VASI (visual approach slope indicator) lights aid pilots in nighttime landing approaches.

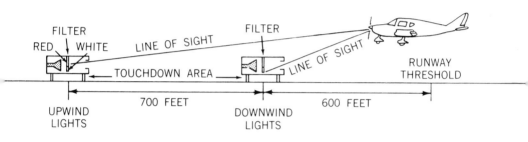

VASI APPROACH

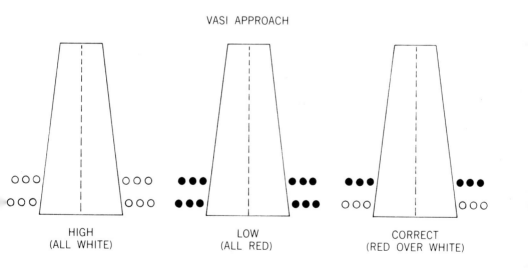

HIGH
(ALL WHITE)

LOW
(ALL RED)

CORRECT
(RED OVER WHITE)

ner, preferably in a well-lighted area with the aid of a flashlight. In addition to being valuable during the preflight inspection, a flashlight becomes very important in case of a malfunction of any of the instrument or cabin lights. So, it's a good idea to take one with you, or keep one in the airplane if you're affluent enough to own one. Some pilots prefer to place a layer of red cellophane between the lens and the bulb to provide red light, which is much less detrimental to night vision.

Owls and cats perform much better at night than humans because their eyes are designed for it. You can make out details better during daylight hours because of the way your eyes are designed.

The retina, or layer of cells at the back of the eyeball that receives light and produces the images you see, is made up of two distinct types of cells called *rods* and *cones*. The cones, and there are millions of them, are in the center area of the retina and are used to detect color, detail and distinct objects. Your top visual acuity occurs when images are sharply focused on a tiny portion of the retina called the *fovea*. The rods, and there are even more of them than cones, are arranged around the cones and pick up color only as shades of gray— much like watching a black-and-white television set. Rods aren't much good for either detail or distance and are the cells that are mostly used at night.

Because of the location of the rods and cones, your method of focusing on objects will be slightly different at night from during the daytime. Since the cones are in the center, most of the detail you see in daylight will be at the point on which you are focusing. But in darkness, because the rods are working and the cones are loafing, you can see an object better by not staring directly at it, but rather slightly to one side.

Your eyes will shift from using cones to rods gradually. As the light decreases, more and more of the rods take over. But the rods need a little time to adapt to the dark. It takes the average person about thirty minutes to fully adapt to night vision. Rods are not as sensitive to red light as white, so cabin lights in most airplanes today are red, although recent studies indicate that a careful blend of blue-white light is better, since red disturbs normal color relationships. It's almost impossible, for example, to read a map with a red light.

Following the preflight inspection, one of the first steps every pilot should take before any night flight is to make sure he is thoroughly familiar with the airplane's cabin, instrumentation and normal layout. Since markings on some switches and circuit breakers may be hard to read at night, the pilot should be able to locate, use these devices and read the markings in poor lighting conditions. Many instructors like to give students what is commonly called a "blindfold cockpit check." This isn't usually done with a blindfold, but the instructor will generally ask you to close your eyes and then ask you to point out certain switches and instruments. You'd be surprised, even after spending several hours flying a certain airplane, how difficult it is to pick them out by memory. To see what I mean, try it in your car, which more than likely has only one tenth as many switches and instruments, even if it happens to be some exotic foreign sports car.

One of the toughest parts of night flying into or out of an unfamiliar airport is taxiing. This is especially true if you haven't been there before during the daytime. Even a familiar airport looks strangely different the first time you try taxiing there at night.

Most airports, including some of the smallest, are equipped with rotating beacons to make them easier to locate at night. Beacons at civilian airports produce alternating green and white flashes, while those identifying military airports emit *two* white flashes alternating with a single green flash.

As you might already have imagined, the painted markings on runways, ramps and taxiways are not much help to pilots at night. Therefore, various types of lighting aids, such as the VASI lights already discussed, are used to mark and identify various segments of the airport for night operations. Taxiways are marked along the edges with blue lights to distinguish them from runways, which have white lights along their borders. The threshold of a runway is marked with six or more green lights and obstructions or displaced thresholds are identified with red lights. Wind indicators such as wind socks, wind tees and tetrahedrons are often lighted to make them visible from the air.

Taxiing at night, even at a well-illuminated airport, can be difficult. About the only advice anyone can give a newcomer is to take it slow and easy *at all times*, and use your landing/taxi light if necessary. But remember, if you do, it will ruin your carefully prepared night vision. The landing light can be used for both landings and takeoffs, but it isn't necessary. And during flight training, instructors usually have their students learn to take off and land at night without using the landing light. This is good training in case the light fails sometime.

Once in the air, most fledgling night pilots find their visual impressions strikingly different from those they are accustomed to in daylight. Most pilots agree that night flying is a *semi-instrument condition.* Yet, despite its limitations, night flying is easier in some respects. The outlines of major cities and towns are clearly discernible, and major metropolitan areas are visible (at least in good weather) from 100 miles away or more, depending on altitude. Major highways tend to stand out at night because of automobile headlights. And on clear moonlit nights the outlines of the terrain and other surface features are dimly visible. (On extremely dark nights, however, terrain features are all but invisible except in brightly lighted populated areas.) Lakes, rivers and the ocean are often easy to see on moonlit nights because of the reflection of the moonlight on the water.

Other airplanes may be easier to see at night, too. Determining which way they're going, however, is another matter. The airplane's navigation or position lights, like a lot of other aviation equipment and terminology, are similar to those of ships. The lighting arrangement (red light on the left wing, green on the right and white light on the tail) can tell you approximately what that other airplane is doing and where it's going. Sailors used the phrase "red right—returning," meaning that when you see the red and green lights of another ship (airplane) and the red light is on the right, the other vessel (airplane) is headed toward you—not necessarily on a collision course, but at least in your general direction.

All recently manufactured aircraft certified for night flight must have anticollision lights to make them easier to see at night. This is most often a red rotating beacon on the top of the tail fin, which can be seen many miles away in good atmospheric conditions. Many pilots turn on this light even in daytime as an added safety factor, especially in congested airspace such as that over large metropolitan areas—particularly on weekends. An increasing number of airplanes are being equipped with brilliant, flashing, white strobe lights which can be seen for even greater distances than the rotating red beacons. Both anticollision lights, however, are useful during daylight flight when rain, clouds, fog or haze reduce visibility.

In some respects, night landings are actually easier than daytime landings, because the air is generally smoother and you don't have disrupting turbulence and crosswinds. Night landings do, however, demand some slightly different techniques. Careful attention is required in flying the landing-approach pattern to make sure you maintain correct altitude. This means monitoring the altimeter and vertical velocity indicator every few seconds to check on your rate of descent. Since judging distances also is more difficult, plan on making a pattern that requires the use of power all the way around—right up to the moment of touchdown. This gives you much better control of the airplane. But don't add too much power—just a squirt above idle is best. The common tendency is to carry too much airspeed on night landings, so the whole process simply requires more refined techniques and concentration. The landing checklist also should be carefully followed, taking even more time than in daylight, to ensure no mistakes.

The aesthetic advantages of night flying are tremendous, and you'll find that after you overcome the slight confusion and apprehension surrounding that first flight after sunset, you'll be sold on night flying. And, perhaps more important, you'll be a much better pilot.

8
The
Pilot
as
Weatherman

Whether transcontinental airline captain or weekend birdman, every pilot must learn to be a good amateur weatherman. Air masses, clouds, storm fronts, high- and low-pressure areas, cloud ceilings, rain, hail and fog quickly become deeply personal ingredients in your environment once you begin learning to fly airplanes. A prediction of rain may warn most people that they'll need a raincoat tomorrow, but to the pilot it may well mean a major change in plans. Like cleaning out the attic instead of making that pleasant cross-country trip. Sometimes those lovely summer days, so perfect for a picnic or outing at the beach or lake, can be rough going in a small airplane if the air is churning with bouncy thermals.

The influence weather has over flying hit home early in my training. After about four or five lessons, a storm front moved in, carrying with it heavy wind and rain. My plans for flying had to be revised daily, and I ended up not flying for more than a week. Since I had so little foundation after such a short time in the airplane, it was practically like starting over again when the weather finally cleared. To most people the surprise storm was a minor aggravation. To me and to fellow student pilots it was a major imposition.

Of course, modern airplanes, radio navigational aids and better weather information have removed most of the hazards and a great deal of the limitations once imposed on pilots, but weather conditions are still a major concern among responsible pilots. Only the very foolhardy will take off on a cross-country flight without checking available weather information about the route and the destination. Just because it's a nice day where you are doesn't mean the same weather conditions exist 500 miles away, or even as little as 50 miles distant. Slight differences in weather conditions from one place to another—such as fog, wind, rain or a cloud ceiling—wouldn't make much difference to the motorist. But to the pilot it might mean canceling or delaying the trip, landing at a different airport or risking your neck.

The most important things about weather for you to know is how to get information and then to be able to understand what you're told. Meteorology is a complicated science for the layman, but there are a few simple rules to follow:

—Don't fly in bad weather.

—Don't fly *into* bad weather.

No pilot with any sense at all would go up when it's stormy or threatening to be. But too many accidents happen because a pilot runs into bad weather and figures he can fly through it and reach his destination. If you're on a cross-country flight and fail to get weather information (which almost always means you've been careless) or, as can happen on rare occasions, get caught by a front moving faster than you figured—you should do one of two things:

—Land at the nearest airport.

—Turn around and head back to where you came from.

You may be delayed a few hours, but you won't be alone. There will probably be a number of other wise pilots in the same predicament, and you can relax together over a cup of coffee and do some "hangar flying" while waiting for the weather to clear.

The National Weather Service maintains a comprehensive weather-observing program and a nationwide aviation weather forecasting service. At some locations, the actual weather observations are made by FAA flight service specialists or by the FAA traffic controllers associated with the airport traffic control towers.

FAA flight service stations are pilot communication centers that provide preflight weather briefing for pilots and scheduled aviation weather broadcasts you can pick up along the route you're following. If an airport has no flight service station or traffic control tower, but does have a Weather Service Airport Station, pilot briefing services are provided by the National Weather Service. The National Weather Service and flight service stations are equipped with a vast communications system, measuring instruments, maps, charts and radar information that help pilots plan trips and avoid getting lost or running into foul weather unexpectedly.

The National Weather Service has stations throughout the United States and coordinates the use of weather information from Canada, Alaska and many ships at sea. These stations are the primary means of determining current weather and predicting future weather conditions. Meteorologists are usually on duty around the clock at most of these stations, making observations and sending hourly reports to central locations. The National Weather Service is responsible for operating the national weather teletypewriter systems.

Along the commercial airways and important areas off the airways, weather observations are taken and transmitted regularly throughout the country via teletype reports. This provides weather stations throughout the country with up-to-date weather information. Each station in a local circuit sends its own report in assigned order. Monitoring stations on the circuit then relay selected reports from other stations, beginning with nearby stations and following with those farther away. In this manner, each station picks up current reports from stations along their own circuit, plus selected reports from other circuits. Reports are usually

Above: Cumulus

Above: Stratus. Below: Stratocumulus

Above: Nimbostratus. Below: Cumulonimbus

One way of classifying clouds is according to how they are formed. Two basic types of clouds are cumulus *and* stratus. *Cumulus clouds are formed by rising air currents and are found in unstable air that favors vertical development. Stratus clouds are formed when a layer of moist air is cooled below its saturation point. These clouds, also referred to as* stratiform *clouds, lie mostly in horizontal layers or sheets.*

transmitted every hour around the clock, except occasional "special" reports if and when the weather may take a drastic or unexpected change.

You too can be a help to weathermen and other pilots by keeping weather stations along your route posted of conditions you find in the air. The sky may be overcast when you take off from an airport, but the weather otherwise dry and the ceiling high enough for most small planes. But when you reach 3000 feet you encounter rain. If you notify the nearest airport (probably the one you just left), this information will be valuable to other pilots who might be planning a cross-country flight, or possibly the student who had planned to put in some solo time practicing advanced maneuvers. You will then be filing a *PIREP*—or pilot report. These timely reports are always the most valuable and current information available. So don't hesitate to share such information.

This sharing of information works two ways. When it becomes apparent to weather forecasters and flight service station personnel that weather conditions in a certain area may be hazardous, or appear to be growing worse than originally forecast, attendants will broadcast weather information over radio navigation frequencies. This is another example of the many ways radio communication has advanced general aviation. These advisories come in two forms, *SIGMETS* and *AIRMETS*.

SIGMETS include information on severe weather conditions that would concern all pilots regardless of their experience, rating and type of aircraft. These conditions include tornadoes, thunderstorms, squall lines, hail three-fourths of an inch in diameter or more, severe and extreme turbulence, severe icing and widespread duststorms or sandstorms which reduce visibility to less than two miles.

AIRMETS are issued for conditions less severe than for SIGMETS. They cover conditions potentially hazardous to airplanes with limited capabilities because of lack of equipment, instrumentation or pilot qualification. AIRMETS warn of moderate icing, moderate turbulence over an extensive area, large areas where visibility is less than two miles or ceilings less than 1000 feet including mountain ridges or passes, and sustained winds of 40 knots at or within 2000 feet of the Earth's surface.

Using these services, and with a basic general knowledge of what to watch out for, any pilot is safe flying anywhere in the United States—assuming he exercises good judgment. But some study of weather, winds and clouds is still necessary.

WEATHER THEORY

There are several factors at work to produce the weather we experience on this planet. Before the space age, scientists believed that weather was primarily the result of the sun's rays hitting the Earth and the reradiation of those rays bouncing off the surface back into the atmosphere. This still appears to account for a majority of our weather, but now meteorologists believe the picture to be much more complex. Increased

Above: Cirrus

Above: Cirrostratus. Below: Cirrocumulus

Above: Altostratus. Below: Altocumulus

Clouds are also named according to their characteristic elevation. Cirrus *clouds are the high clouds normally found above
20,000 feet. Because these clouds are found in the cold air at
high elevations, they are composed of ice-crystals and take on
a thin, wispy appearance.* Alto-*prefixed clouds are the middle
clouds found between 6,500 feet and 16,500 feet. Clouds without either of these two prefixes are low clouds normally found
below 6,500 feet.*

radiation from the sun, electrical charges in the atmosphere and even the ocean currents all play a role in the wonder of weather.

Approximately 85 percent of the heat present in the atmosphere is created by the reradiation process, while about 15 percent is produced by the direct rays of the sun as they pass through the atmosphere on their way to the Earth. But this heating process isn't equal over the entire surface. Various kinds of terrain, such as mountains, flat desert areas, trees, lakes and so forth, all influence how much reradiation takes place.

One major reason for uneven heating is the different angles at which the sun's rays strike the Earth's surface. These rays reach the earth almost directly—or at about a 90-degree angle—at the equator, which makes this sunshine the most intense anywhere on earth. As the air along the equator heats, it also expands and rises. This produces low-pressure areas at the equator, so cooler air from the polar regions moves in to fill the void. This process sets up a current of air masses circulating around the globe, with the warm air fanning out toward the North and South Poles and then returning along the surface to the equator.

As this air circulates, the flow is controlled and changed by the oceans, the land masses, the rotation of the Earth and by low-pressure zones created by highly heated land areas.

A high-pressure area usually means good weather, while a low-pressure system indicates bad conditions. But you still need more information about weather than a pressure reading. There are five types of pressure systems you will hear or read about as a pilot:

1. *Low*—An area of low pressure is like a depression or a valley in the atmosphere.
2. *High*—It can be visualized as a mountain surrounded by valleys or areas of low pressure on all sides.
3. *Trough*—This is an elongated area of relatively low pressure, extending from the center of a low-pressure system.
4. *Ridge*—The high-pressure equivalent of a trough.
5. *Col*—This is a neutral area between two high-pressure or low-pressure areas.

If it were not for the rotation of the Earth, air would constantly move directly from high-pressure areas to low-pressure areas. This rotation, however, deflects the air toward the right in the Northern Hemisphere, and toward the left in the Southern Hemisphere. It is from this deflection process that we have our continuous prevailing winds. Air moving around the high-pressure system at the North Pole circulates clockwise and moves outward from the center of the high. This produces the prevailing wind system known as the *polar easterlies.* (Remember that wind directions are labeled according to the direction *from* which they are blowing.)

At 60 degrees north latitude, south to 30 degrees north latitude, which encompasses most of the United States and Canada, the air circulation is counterclockwise, producing the *prevailing westerlies.* From 30 degrees north latitude south to the equator, air circu-

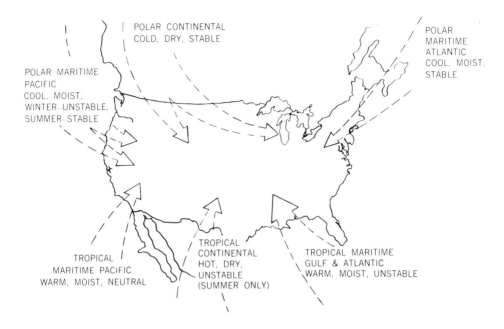

Air masses and their source regions.

lates clockwise and produces the *northeast trade winds.*

Because of the prevailing westerlies, a pilot flying from San Francisco to New York will almost always get a little boost from a tail wind, while a pilot on the reverse route will have to buck a head wind.

Most of the weather conditions we encounter each day—whether good or bad—are the result of certain air masses that drift across the Earth's surface, or the interaction between two or more of these air masses. This interaction is called a *front.* But again, there will always be variations caused by differences in terrain. Air masses inherit their traits from the regions over which they are formed. Those created in the polar regions, for example, are called *polar,* and are cold. The warm *tropical* air masses are formed in regions close to the equator. Air masses formed over land are usually relatively dry and are known as *continental* air masses. *Maritime* air masses originate over large bodies of water and will carry considerable moisture. Since there are few absolutes in weather (which most of us are well aware of), you may hear about various combinations of these, such as *maritime polar* air masses.

Air masses may be further identified according to their place of origin, such as Atlantic, Pacific or Gulf. But their most common description (especially on the evening news show) will be either *warm* or *cold*. Cold air masses (or fronts) usually bring with them turbulence and when enough moisture is present thunderstorms, hail, sleet and even snow flurries. Warm fronts generally produce much milder weather, although they are often accompanied by fog, drizzles and bad visibility in the lower atmosphere when smoke and dust are present—which is often the case over large cities and industrial areas. When air masses encounter one another, the result is something akin to that old game called King of the Mountain. If a cold air mass is advancing toward a warm air mass, the cold, heavy air attempts to push under and lift up the warm, relatively lighter air. Conversely, a warm air mass, advancing toward cold retreating air, pushes up over the cold air. It's generally this pushing and shoving that stirs up most of the nasty weather. Sometimes, though, there will be a standoff. If the boundary between the two air masses does not move, you have what meteorologists call, simply, a *stationary* front.

Large bodies of water often have considerable effect

on weather conditions. During the winter, the Great Lakes are warmer than the surrounding land areas and the cold air masses that move southward from Canada. This is because land heats up and cools off faster than water. So, both heat and moisture are added to these cold air masses as they pass over the lakes. The resulting convection—or upward movement of warm air into cold—produces the kind of nasty wind, rain and snow flurries that people in that part of the country complain about and describe in songs. Few pilots, however, would find much to sing about in that kind of weather!

Likewise, the uneven heating of land and water is instrumental in creating the sea breezes usually encountered along coastal areas during the day. As the land heats up in daylight hours, the warm air begins rising in convection currents. This leaves a void, and the cooler, heavier sea air rushes in to fill the growing empty space, creating the cool marine breezes that help keep temperatures down at the beach on hot days. At night the reverse takes place. As the ground begins to cool faster than the ocean, a low-pressure area develops over the water and the cooler inland air rushes out to sea causing what is known as, appropriately, land breezes.

Terrain also has a major effect on the movement of air masses and currents. When the wind blows against a mountain, the moisture content of the air and its stability determine the amount and height of clouds, their thickness and their nature. Fronts and low-pressure systems, when moving through mountainous regions, create more cloudiness and rain, turbulence and icing conditions on the windward slopes than when moving over flat terrain. This is because the terrain lifting effect is added to the frontal lifting forces already at work.

The movement of air over mountain ranges can often create tremendous turbulence and hazardous conditions for light aircraft. Air, being cooled and forced up over a mountain, has a tendency to roll and tumble down the leeward side of the mountain causing tremendous downdrafts. It also causes a wave or rippling motion in the atmosphere that can extend for miles downwind from the mountain range. These powerful air currents are known as *mountain waves* and are capable of producing severe downdrafts in excess of 5000 feet per minute! It is important for pilots to avoid being caught in such predicaments, which can quickly end in disaster. Cloud formations will give you a good clue to turbulent conditions over mountains. A lenticular cloud, which is a lens-shaped cloud, is usually found at the top of these mountain waves. At about the same level as the mountain peak, or the ridge of the mountain range, roll or rotor clouds, which can look like a tornado funnel turned on its side, will form. If you spot these, better either alter your route, if possible, or make a 180-degree turn. A light airplane caught in a mountain wave can quickly be thrown out of control and plummet into the mountainside.

Even gentle rolling hills can make rough going in a small airplane at only 2000 or 3000 feet. The combination of convection currents rising off the ground, plus the rolling motion of the air as it actually bounces and tumbles over hills, creates up- and downdrafts that can toss a small airplane around like a rubber lifeboat in the crashing surf.

By contrast, if you happen to be flying over water, the air will be smooth. Likewise, flying over forests or flat farmland is always smoother than hilly or mountainous country. But a patch of trees or a cluster of buildings near the head of the runway will create an updraft on warm days and you will "bounce" a little as you glide over them on a landing approach. These are all things a good pilot is aware of, to prevent being caught in a dangerous situation.

Convection currents rising off the earth produce dramatic differences in the way your airplane will handle. If you happen to be trying to land on a hot day on an approach over empty fields, the updrafts will push you beyond your touchdown spot unless you take them into account. On the other hand, if you are approaching over water, the convection currents will drag you down somewhat, and unless you compensate for this by adding necessary power, you could very easily touch down short of the runway.

Clouds are about the best "signposts" you'll find in the sky. Their location and appearance (size, shape and color) can show a weather-wise aviator where turbulence might be found, whether a frontal system is approaching or where hail might be encountered. It is often possible, through experience, to read the existing weather situation, and how it may change, by watching the clouds.

The first thing a student pilot must remember about clouds, however, is that it's sometimes okay to fly over them, under them or around them—but never *through* them! Save such adventure for when you earn that instrument ticket. And even instrument-rated pilots will avoid flying "blind" through clouds if it's at all reasonable. Your visibility is almost always limited to a few feet beyond the airplane—and that's insane at 100-plus miles per hour! During the course of instruction for the private license you'll be required to fly some under the hood as I've already described, but that is training for an emergency situation only—not license to buzz around through the clouds. A slight misjudgment about your altitude or location could end your fun abruptly. And it is incredibly easy to get disoriented when you are unable to see beyond the propeller.

Cloud types are separated into four families: high, middle, low and clouds with large vertical development. They are further broken down according to their form and appearance. Puffy or billowy clouds are *cumulus*, the layered types are *stratus*. If there is rain, *nimbo* (meaning rain) is added to the name, as in *nimbostratus* or *cumulonimbus*.

Cumulus clouds are formed by rising air currents and are found in unstable air. The currents of air create clouds with a piled-up or bunched appearance. Stratus clouds are formed when a layer of moist air is cooled below its saturation point. Stratiform clouds lie mostly in horizontal layers or sheets, resisting vertical development.

The prefixes and suffixes which are combined to make up the names of clouds tell something important about their character. Nimbus, as already mentioned, indicates the presence of some form of precipitation— rain, snow or hail. Broken or fragmented clouds are prefixed by *fracto*, such as *fractostratus* or *fractocumulus*. Lenticular clouds, which we've already discussed, are formed over mountains during high wind conditions and have a lens-shaped appearance.

Elevation also is used to categorize clouds. *Cirrus* clouds are the high clouds normally found above 20,000 feet. Because these clouds are found in the cold air at high elevations, they are composed of ice crystals and take on a thin, wispy appearance. Clouds with the prefix *alto* are the middle clouds found between 6500 feet and 16,500 feet. Clouds without either of these two prefixes are low clouds normally circulating below 6500 feet.

High clouds are composed almost entirely of ice crystals because of the extremely cold temperatures at higher altitudes. These clouds include cirrus, cirrocumulus and cirrostratus. The bases of the high clouds average about 25,000 feet, but present no icing hazard to airplanes. Generally, these clouds are so thin that the outline of the sun or moon may be seen through them, which produces the halo effect you've probably seen many times.

Altocumulus and altostratus are the middle cloud group. Altocumulus clouds can form in several different ways and take on various appearances. Generally, however, they are patchy layers of puffy, roll-like clouds of a whitish or grayish color. They often resemble cirrocumulus, but the puffs or rolls are much larger. Instead of being made of ice crystals, middle clouds consist mostly of very small water droplets. Altocumulus clouds are a good indication of unfavorable flying conditions. Altostratus clouds are simply stratus clouds that form in the middle altitudes.

Low clouds consist of stratus, stratocumulus and nimbostratus. These formations are the most important ones to private pilots because they create low ceilings and visibility limits close to the ground. Their base, or what would be called the ceiling, can change rapidly. When any of these lower clouds drop to within 50 feet of the ground, we call them *fog.*

The stratus cloud has a uniform base and a dull gray appearance, resembling fog. Stratus clouds make the sky appear heavy and will occasionally produce fine drizzles or very light snow and fog. Since there is little or no vertical building with stratus clouds, they rarely produce heavy rain or snow.

The real rain- or snow-producing clouds are nimbostratus, which are much darker in appearance than ordinary stratus clouds. These are the thick clouds that usually produce continuous rain, snow or sleet.

Puffy, rolling white layers of clouds are stratocumulus, and rarely produce any rain by themselves, but sometimes develop into cumulonimbus—or thunderheads. These clouds are characterized by violent updrafts which carry the tops of the clouds to extreme altitudes—sometimes as high as 75,000 feet. Tornadoes, hail and severe rainstorms are all products of this type

Thundercloud-building activity as viewed from the air.

of cloud formation. At the top of the cloud, a flat anvil-shaped thunderhead caused by the powerful updrafts will form as the cloud begins to dissipate.

If you're flying in the vicinity of a thunderstorm, you can be sucked into violent conditions with winds up to 150 mph that would literally rip a small airplane apart. And if your airplane isn't ripped apart, it could very well be pelleted to pieces by giant hailstones.

Remember that it's impossible for a small plane to fly above these mindless machines of destruction. Scooting under them is also difficult, if not impossible, because of the violent winds and heavy rain. And trying to skirt around them is often risky because they move so fast and their tentacles extend so many miles you might suddenly find yourself trapped on all sides. Your only sensible option is to land as soon as possible or turn around and head the other way. If you're foolish enough to ever get caught in a thunderstorm, throttle back to below cruising speed (generally between 90 and 100 mph in most light planes) to reduce the chance of serious structural damage to the airplane.

Like the cumulonimbus or thunderhead, lightning is no friend of the pilot.

Perhaps the most common weather restriction for pilots is fog. In some parts of the country fog is a fairly rare experience, but along coastal areas it is a frequent unwanted intruder in the life of an airman.

Since fog is a dense stratiform cloud hanging within 50 feet of the Earth's surface, visibility can be reduced to almost nil. And even if visibility is as much as a hundred yards—that's not a lot when you're trying to land an airplane. Even a veteran airplane captain would balk at that situation. That's why it's important for any pilot to check weather conditions at his destination before leaving on a flight. If you should run into fog, you very well might not be able to land, and it could be a long way to another airport. And should your fuel supply be low, you'd be in real trouble.

You can expect fog—or should be prepared for it—when the temperature and dew point are within 4 degrees Fahrenheit. The dew point is simply the temperature at which air can no longer contain moisture. For every 20-degree (Fahrenheit) increase in temperature, the air doubles its humidity capacity. Each time the temperature drops 20 degrees, the capacity of air to hold water is cut in half. For instance, if you knew the temperature was 70 degrees and the relative humidity (dew point) is 50 percent, then a drop of 20 degrees in temperature will bring with it some kind of condensation in the form of either rain or fog. Humidity is the word we are most familiar with, but the pilot reading weather charts or phoning the weather service will receive the information as temperature 70 degrees, dew point 50.

The high relative humidity necessary for fog can occur in two ways: when the air is cooled to its dew point or when moisture is added to the air near the surface. Another necessary ingredient for the formation of fog is an abundance of what meteorologists call *condensation nuclei,* which are particles of salt or smoke suspended in the atmosphere providing the nuclei around which water vapor can cling and then

Hurricane Carmen as seen by satellite at 2 p.m., September 7, 1974, when the storm was 150 miles south of Louisiana and directly south of New Orleans, packing winds of 150 miles per hour, with gusts of 175 mph.

condense. A light surface wind is also necessary for fog formation, since it provides a mixing action which spreads and increases the thickness of fog. But a strong wind will break up the fog layer and chase the stratus clouds away.

Weather conditions will always influence—and sometimes hamper—flying. But as forecasts have become more accessible and timely, airplanes more reliable and sophisticated and pilots better informed, weather is less a threat today than in years past. The pilot who studies weather, knows what to look for and keeps alert is unlikely to ever run into any serious trouble. Take those extra few minutes to check forecasts before leaving on a flight and check in either via radio or along the way as you stop. You'll find that forecasters love to talk about the weather even more than the guy on the street, and they respect the pilot who wants all the details. So there's no reason to feel that you're being a pest if you ask a lot of questions. Those questions can very well prevent unpleasant and unexpected landings later on.

9

Examination Day

Although most flight schools will tell you it's possible to earn the private ticket in 40 hours, the national average is much closer to 60. And while it might impress your friends to tell them you did it in the minimum time, chances are you'll be much better prepared for the test and be a better pilot if you have more than 40 or 45 hours in your logbook.

To earn the private license you must pass *three tests:* First, the FAA written, a three-hour monster of 60 multiple-choice questions covering the entire range of your training; second, an oral exam by an FAA flight examiner and, third, the actual flight test itself where you demonstrate your ability to perform all the maneuvers and various piloting skills you've been practicing so diligently.

The written exam, although tricky, isn't as difficult as some people may tell you. To pass it requires good preparation and thought. The written test is meant to judge your knowledge of the rules and regulations set up by the FAA for weather, map work, flight planning and all of the material available to the pilot and necessary for safe flying. It seems tough, and it *is*. But the FAA says there are no trick questions, and there are none. The trick is to know exactly how to find the answer with your computer or on paper, exactly how to use your *Airman's Information Manual, Flight Information Manual,* sectional charts, read weather reports and draw on all the knowledge you're supposed to have absorbed during your training. You need a score of 70 or better to pass the test, which means 42 of the 60 questions have to be answered correctly. For those who are prepared, three hours is ample time to complete the test and double-check your answers. So there's no need to rush.

To prepare for the examination, students can choose from several options. The training programs designed by aircraft manufacturers integrate flight instruction with preparation for the written exam. By means of periodic quizzes and workbook exercises, the student is able to practice with the material included in the test. These courses even include a sample exam in the FAA format.

Less structured training programs offer ground

school, which is usually conducted in a classroom by a certified flight and/or ground instructor. The students are generally in various phases of flight training. Most ground schools make use of audiovisual aids and a companion course. Their essential difference from the manufacturer's dealer programs is a lack of synchronization with each step of flight training. For example, you may be in the process of mastering takeoffs and landings, while studying navigation in ground school.

One of the major advantages of manufacturer's audiovisual training programs is that you can study at your own pace and convenience. For a working person on a busy schedule, this is a big plus. There are also many home-study courses and books that can more than adequately prepare you for the test. If you elect to go this route, you'll undoubtedly set up periods of ground briefing with your instructor to clarify any questions you may have and arrange to have periodic checks of what you have covered.

Another program is the weekend course. Highly touted for people with a minimum of spare time, such courses are set up as "clinics" around the country. The classroom training is intensive—all the material for the exam is covered in two days. Those who receive the greatest benefit from these courses are people who have already been through all or most of the material without having taken the exam and who want a thorough review first.

At the start of the examination, you'll be given the owner's manual of an airplane, which will contain the information pertinent to its operation, and a sectional chart. You also will be told what the weather conditions for a theoretical trip will be and asked questions about the trip you plan. These questions are intended to test your ability to handle weather, navigation and the performance characteristics of your airplane within the framework of the appropriate regulations, and thus conduct a safe flight.

In about 10 days to three weeks, the FAA will mail you your score and list the subject areas you had trouble with, so you may review them prior to the oral exam that is the next stage of your private pilot test.

Some sample questions are listed below. They are taken from the *FAA Private Pilot Written Examination Guide,* which is available from the Superintendent of Documents, U.S. Government Printing Office, Washington, D.C. 20402. The answers, along with a brief discussion of them, follow each question. See how many you can answer.

1. When flying cross-country your best choice during preflight planning for VFR should be:
   (1) Sectional chart.
   (2) World Aeronautical Chart.
   (3) Radio facility.
   (4) Route chart.

   (1) Sectional charts are always the best choice for private pilots on VFR flight, except in rare cases where you may be traveling long distances and not want to carry a load of charts.

2. For VFR flight in a control area, the minimum flight visibility and proximity to cloud requirements are:
   (1) Visibility 3 miles; 500 feet under, 1000 feet over and 2000 feet horizontally from the clouds.
   (2) Visibility 3 miles; clear of the clouds.
   (3) Visibility 1 mile; 500 feet under, 1000 feet over, 2000 feet horizontally from the clouds.
   (4) Visibility 1 mile; clear of the clouds.

   (1) These requirements are found in the Federal Aviation Regulations, Part 91.105: "Basic VFR weather minimums."

3. The principal source of weather conditions between reporting stations is from:
   (1) Weather sequence reports.
   (2) Pilot reports en route (PIREPs).
   (3) FAA control towers.
   (4) Commercial broadcasting stations.

   (2) PIREPs are always the most current information available to fellow pilots.

4. *The most* important rule to remember in the event of a power failure on takeoff after becoming airborne is to:
   (1) Maintain safe airspeed.
   (2) Gain altitude immediately.
   (3) Turn back to the takeoff field.
   (4) Determine the wind direction.

(1) A successful emergency landing is usually possible if touchdown is made with the aircraft in a level attitude and at a reduced but safe airspeed. Attempting to return to the airport would require a steep turn resulting in a drastic loss of altitude.

5. The most important reason for servicing fuel tanks to full capacity upon completion of a flight is because this procedure:
   (1) Prevents drying and cracking of the inner fuel cell liner that occurs when the liner is exposed to the air.
   (2) Minimizes the possibility of corrosion and structural damage due to moisture forming on and dripping from the outer walls of the fuel tanks.
   (3) Prevents the fuel evaporation that occurs in partially filled tanks.
   (4) Minimizes the possibility of fuel contamination from condensation of water on inner walls of partially filled tanks.

(4) Answers 1 and 3 may pertain to partially filled tanks, but they should not be considered the primary reason for fueling after each flight or at the end of the day.

6. In level flight at a steady airspeed:
   (1) Thrust exceeds gravity.
   (2) Thrust exceeds drag.
   (3) Lift equals gravity.
   (4) Lift exceeds the weight of an airplane.

(3) Answers 2 and 4 may be true, technically, but the main principle involved here, as discussed in Chapter 1, is that lift equals gravity.

7. While in flight you hit an area of turbulence, so you slow your speed to one where sudden changes in attitude can be made more safely. This speed is designated as:
   (1) Never-exceed speed.
   (2) Flap speed.
   (3) Maneuvering speed.
   (4) Maximum structural cruising speed.

(3) The maneuvering speed may be different in each airplane, so it's up to the pilot to familiarize himself with the airplane he's flying.

8. As part of preflight planning, you correct your known true course for wind drift, variation and deviation. The result of these corrections is:
   (1) Compass heading.
   (2) Magnetic heading.
   (3) True heading.
   (4) Compass course.

(1) This is an example of how the test can be tricky. If this question threw you, better go back and review Chapter 6 on cross-country flight. The key to taking the written examination is to read each question slowly and carefully before answering it. One answer is likely to be obviously wrong, another very probably wrong, a third an "educated

mistake" (these are the ones especially to watch out for) and the fourth undeniably correct. With adequate preparation, the test can be an enjoyable challenge. Without adequate preparation, it will seem like three hours with the devil. The FAA isn't out to flunk you, but rather to ensure that you have the ability and knowledge to meet the demands and responsibilities of being a pilot. And they are many.

After you have passed the written test, and reviewed any areas where you may be a little weak, it's then time to make an appointment with an FAA flight examiner for the actual flight test. If you live in a fairly large metropolitan area and took lessons at one of the bigger schools, there will probably be an examiner on the staff. Chances are, in that case, you already know the person, which may go a long way in reducing your nervousness on examination day. But probably not much. No matter how confident we are of our piloting skills, when we walk out to the airplane with that examiner, our confidence seems to fall apart. It's a rare person, indeed, who feels calm and collected. The examiner knows that, too.

The private flight test consists of three phases: the oral examination, basic piloting skills and cross-country flying.

On the oral exam you'll be expected to present and explain the required documents in the airplane being used on the flight test. These include the Airworthiness Certificate, Airplane Flight Manual, Registration Certificate and the aircraft and engine logbooks. You'll also have to know the airplane's performance, range and mechanical operation. This means understanding and being able to explain the fuel, electric and hydraulic systems. No one expects you to be an engineer, but you are expected to know more about your airplane than most motorists unfortunately know about their cars. Know the effects of altitude and temperature on aircraft performance. And study Federal Aviation Regulations 61 and 91 *thoroughly*. Every item in these regulations pertains to you as a private pilot.

After the oral quiz, which may take from 30 minutes to an hour, you'll then be asked to plot a cross-country course, figuring magnetic heading, wind drift, fuel consumption and how long the trip will take. When that's finished, the check pilot will escort you out to the airplane and watch you carefully as you make your preflight external check. In all probability he (or often she) will ask you questions about the airplane, what you're doing and why. Be prepared to give concise and complete answers.

This oral examination counts heavily in the final outcome of the flight test. Too many students go into the flight test unprepared, or thinking they can bluff their way through, and find they've flunked the test before they even leave the ground.

The actual flight part of the test will cover everything you've been practicing as a student—coordinated turns, stalls, slow flight, crosswind, short- and soft-field landings and turns around a point. And those low-altitude turns around a point are a likely place to have an emergency thrown at you—so be prepared and scout the ground below at all times. You should have that habit anyway.

During the entire test you'll be judged on your techniques from the moment you shout clear and fire up the engine until you park and shut it off. The check pilot will observe and rate your starting, warm-up, taxi and takeoff skills, and even how efficiently you use the radio.

And bring along a hood. Sometime during the check flight the examiner will expect you to demonstrate how well you can fly the airplane by instruments alone. Don't be surprised if he takes over the controls while you're under the hood and puts the airplane in some predicament like a shallow turning dive or a near stall attitude and then tells you to set things straight. You'll most certainly be asked to make 90- and 180-degree turns and then wind up on a specified heading by sole reference to instruments. Satisfactory performance on this will be safe and positive manual control, not precision in speed, altitude and direction control. However, if you let the airplane get away from you and accidentally assume an unsafe attitude, the examiner might flunk you on this part of the test.

The flight test usually will begin with you conducting the planned cross-country, and the examiner will probably have you fly about 20 to 30 minutes of it to see how well you planned things, picked checkpoints, and if you have the scoop on navigation in general, including use of any radio navigation aids. He'll also probably throw an emergency at you or require a flight to an alternate airport. You'll then have to pick one out, establish a heading toward it within 10 minutes and have a heading accuracy of within 15 degrees.

The flight portion usually takes about 90 minutes on the average and ideally winds up with the examiner turning to you with the warmest smile you've ever seen, and saying, "Congratulations," as he signs your temporary private ticket.

And at that moment you'll be flying higher than ever.

10
Mayday!
Mayday!

If there is one thing few pilots are expert at, it's making forced landings. The reason is simple—modern airplanes are so reliable that mechanical failure is rare. But emergencies are no joking matter, and any questions the aspiring or student pilot has about them will always be answered in a no-nonsense manner. Only a fool would snicker at a fellow pilot's concern about safety.

Emergencies do occur, and when they do, the pilot had better know *what* to do. If the engine quits in your family car, you can coast to the side of the road and grumble about your misfortune. It doesn't come off that easily in an airplane. An engine failure while flying demands quick action, piloting skill and a cool head.

A few years ago, it was decided that more accidents were caused while students were practicing forced landings than there were actual forced landings. This led to the present philosophy that students should be taught emergency procedures without actually making a complete landing.

Sometime during your training, chances are your instructor will, without warning, pull back on the throttle and say, "Forced landing." The idea is to condition you to respond and act promptly and efficiently in an emergency.

Flight requires two major components—airplane and pilot. Although neither is perfect, the human is more likely to be the weaker element. This is partly because the pilot has a tougher job. The airplane has only to continue being what it was before it left the ground. But the pilot has to think, make numerous decisions, navigate, read maps, talk on the radio, watch where he's going—and watch where other airplanes (or pilots) are going—coordinate controls, observe weather conditions and know what to do if the airplane fails at its job. Meanwhile, the airplane simply responds (at least, about 99.99 percent of the time) to orders from the pilot.

Even in those isolated situations where something does go wrong, quick and proper action on the part of the pilot can still bring them both down safely.

Statistics show that airplanes flown within their

limitations (and the pilot's) are almost never completely responsible for accidents. But exceeding these limitations is much like driving a vintage car over an ice-covered mountain road at 100 mph—maybe you'll make it, and maybe you won't. But the odds aren't in your favor.

Most accidents, according to FAA officials, occur as a result of foolhardy flying on the part of the person at the controls. A few pilots, like some motorists, seem to be an accident looking for a place to happen. Some pilots seem destined for disaster by drinking and flying, exhibiting little respect for severe weather, sloppy navigation or flagrant disregard for the airplane's limitations.

No one has ever built a perfect machine. Proof of this can be found in the number of appliance repair and automobile service shops listed in the *Yellow Pages* of all phone books. Even so, most mechanical failures are the result of negligence. An engine rarely conks out without some warning symptoms many hours before it finally quits altogether or begins sputtering along on one or two cylinders with a corresponding loss in power. Regular checks of the instruments will usually warn a pilot of pending trouble—like loss of oil pressure—in enough time to find an airport and put down before the engine seizes up or swallows the valves.

More often a *pilot* fails his engine by letting it run out of gas. If a pilot verifies by visual inspection before a flight that his airplane has enough fuel for a certain number of hours in the air, plans his trip accordingly and then checks his fuel gauges regularly, there is no reason for being caught short. Absolutely none. But you'd be amazed at the number of so-called experienced pilots that plan a five-hour cross-country trip with five-hours' worth of fuel, then get hit with a headwind and run short of fuel.

All airplanes—from Piper Cubs to giant Boeing 747 airliners—are nothing more than powered gliders. When a pilot decides to descend, he does so by pulling back on the throttle and reducing the engine's power to idle. In essence, it is just like letting off the accelerator in your car and coasting down a long hill. Even from an altitude of only 3000 or 4000 feet a pilot who doesn't panic can glide his airplane for several miles before it reaches the bottom of that hill. But panic is all too often what shorts out the pilot's brain.

An alert pilot is always on the lookout for suitable forced-landing sites. The best bet is always an airport— and there are enough of them around today to make this likely in a good many emergencies. The next best alternative would be a long, smooth field with a hard surface. In many areas these may be rare, so the pilot will have to move down the list and find *someplace* that looks long enough to set his airplane down with a minimum of damage to both airplane and passengers.

You should look for a place that is wide enough to allow you to correct for errors in speed, altitude and judgment. The best rule of thumb is to pick a spot within a 45-degree angle from an imaginary vertical line beneath the airplane. The main reason for this is not that the airplane would fail to reach a site farther away, but that a spot that distant may be deceiving. When the pilot glides in for a landing, he may find that his choice for an emergency landing, instead of being flat and smooth, is rimmed with trees or other obstructions, and criss crossed with fences.

Streets, roads and highways may be your only alternative, but they should be a last resort. Traffic, power lines and a narrow width make these arteries hazardous for emergency landings.

The first thing to do if engine failure strikes is to maintain altitude by pulling back slightly on the control wheel to set up your glide speed. This is usually about 80 mph in most light aircraft. Next, scan the area below for the place you're going to set her down. Wind direction is important, too, since it normally is best to land into the wind—although a longer field downwind might be a better choice than a short field into the wind.

Wind direction can be determined in several ways— dust, grass or grain fields that bend with the wind, ripples in a pond or lake and smoke drifting from a chimney or factory. Smoke is probably the best indicator, since it will tell you more about how strong the wind is. If smoke rises slowly and then drifts off, there is a mild wind condition. But if it rises and then abruptly parallels the ground, the surface wind is strong.

Once you've set up a glide and have picked both a place to land and know which direction to approach from, you should quickly run through an emergency checklist. I know this may sound crazy, but you will

If you're lucky enough to find some smoke like this, it will make things a lot easier on a simulated emergency landing—or the real thing, too.

almost always have time and it can possibly save you from having to carry out the emergency landing. According to seasoned flight instructors and other experts in aviation, such a checklist should only take from 10 to 15 seconds. That means, if your airplane is in the correct glide, you will only lose about 100 feet.

There is no hard and fast rule about when this checklist should be performed. Some instructors prefer you to run through it before looking for a landing site, while others insist you should spot the place you're going to land before wasting any more time. Either way, do it soon. As mentioned earlier, complete and immediate power failures are almost always the result of running out of fuel. It would, at the very least, be embarrassing to make a forced landing only to discover that you could have continued on your way if you had only switched the fuel selector to the tank with gas in it! And that has happened many times.

Usually, any sudden engine power loss is caused by some kind of fuel problem. Turn on the electric fuel pump, then check to make sure the fuel selector is set on the correct tank. Next, the mixture should be checked to see if it is in the *rich* position. Carburetor

To make a forced landing, pick a place that's flat and offers ample roll-out room.

heat should then be applied to find out if ice has formed and to clear it out. Then the magneto switch should be checked to see that it is in the *both* position. If none of these checks reveals the cause of the power failure, quickly scan other instruments and make a general inspection inside the cabin to see if the trouble comes from some other source. When the trouble is discovered (if it is) and corrected, the engine will automatically start again without using the ignition because of the "windmilling" effect (spinning) of the propeller.

Once the engine returns to life, don't jam the throttle full forward immediately—open it slowly. If you've glided along from 3000 feet down to about 600 feet, the engine may have cooled off, and ramming the throttle all the way on may cause it to sputter and misfire. If it seems a little balky, give it a shot of primer and then feed the throttle on slowly. One quick shot is usually all that's needed. In hot weather the engine will have a tendency to load up during extended glides and will require careful clearing.

If a thorough check fails to reveal the trouble, take a deep breath and remember that this unplanned and unexpected emergency landing doesn't have to be too much different from any other. Avoid any steep banking that will cause excessive and unwanted loss of altitude. If you are lucky enough to spot a good landing spot directly below, let the airplane spiral down gracefully in lazy 360-degree circles until reaching an altitude that will allow you to set up a normal landing pattern—complete with downwind, base and final leg.

Skimming in over those trees is where all that short-field landing practice pays off. Pull on full flaps, but make sure you've got plenty of airspeed and altitude first.

But again, make sure you maintain proper glide speed to avoid losing too much altitude too soon.

If the best landing spot is a few miles away, try to put the airplane into a glide that will at least wind up where you can enter the base leg. Following a left-hand pattern is always preferred, but it isn't always possible. The most important thing is to visualize some kind of landing pattern and keep in mind that the more you turn this emergency into a normal landing, the better off you'll be right up to the moment the airplane rolls to a stop.

Full flaps should always be used on the final approach, but don't pull them on too soon or you may lose too much airspeed—and in a real emergency you might not be able to add the power necessary to reach that touchdown point.

Occasionally you hear about airplanes crashing on takeoff, and before I started flying I always thought the simple solution to a power failure near the airport would be to make a 180-degree turn and glide back to the runway.

No way!

If a power failure occurs after you've already cleared the end of the runway, but before you've reached about 1000 feet or more, the only thing to do is run through your checklist and then look for a place to land either straight ahead or slightly to one side of your flight path.

In the process of turning around, the airplane will probably lose 300 feet or more. You'll still be too far from the airport—and nowhere near lined up with the runway. To bring the point home hard, during one of our emergency landing sessions, Phyllis pulled the control wheel back hard, and then put the Cherokee into a steep bank as she made a tight 180. All this, fortunately, was done at 1000 feet. When the turn was completed, I glanced at the altimeter. It read just a shade less than 600 feet! In a power-loss emergency you can't afford to lose that much altitude that quickly—but especially not when you're less than 1000 feet. I guess the urge to return to the airport is almost instinctive. But fight it.

And speaking of takeoffs—don't take them for granted. So much attention in flying is given to landings that too many pilots assume the takeoff is just a routine task.

If you had a dime for every word said and written about landings you could probably afford to buy a new airplane. But if you had a dollar for every word uttered about taking off you probably couldn't afford to put gas in that airplane. Takeoff complacency may even contribute to there being nearly as many serious accidents in the takeoff and initial climb phases of flight as happen during approaches and landings. And while mechanical problems should be the only reason for takeoff mishaps, only about 10 percent of takeoff crashes happen because something went wrong with the airplane.

The real culprit in this case appears to be mishandling of the airplane during the takeoff-roll and the initial climb—usually in a crosswind, although some pilots manage to lose control even in ideal conditions. Such accidents seem to happen most frequently during winter and early spring, when crosswinds are strongest.

The best way to make a good—and safe—takeoff in a crosswind is to line up the airplane with the white centerline on the runway. This will serve as a sort of steering guide as the airplane picks up speed. By applying aileron to the windward side you keep the wings level and prevent any sideload from developing. The airplane should then be allowed to accelerate beyond the normal lift-off speed to gain a better rate of climb and prevent stalling.

One mistake that can lead to control troubles during a crosswind takeoff is forcing the wheels on the runway past the normal takeoff speed by pushing the control wheel forward. This will concentrate too much weight on the front wheel—and there's no way of controlling an airplane when the weight's concentrated on the single nosewheel. The tail-dragger pilot has it a little easier. He can raise the tail early in the run to shift the weight to the main landing gear until the airplane lifts off. But the pilot of most tri-gear airplanes can't do anything to put more weight on the main wheels— he can only work at not putting *less* on them.

Another misadventure that is responsible for more than its share of bumps, bruises and expensive repair bills is the *ground loop*. Although most ground loops happen on landings, quite a few pilots manage them on takeoffs too. Several years ago, when tail draggers were still the most common airplane in general aviation, it was axiomatic that there were two kinds of pilots— those who had ground looped an airplane and those who would. It's not quite that bad today, but ground loops are still a problem.

Airplanes with tail wheels are more prone to ground loops, but the tri-gear setup hasn't eliminated the problem, even though it was supposed to. Ground loops in today's aircraft, according to the Flight Safety Foundation, account for at least 15 percent of the total accidents, and they're the second most prevalent type of accident. Since there are many more airplanes equipped with tricycle landing gear today than the tail-wheel variety, it's obvious that the tri-gear airplane can still get you into trouble—if abused.

Essentially, a ground loop is the same thing as a spin out in auto racing, except that the ground loop is somewhat more complex. And, whereas the race driver can come out of a spin without serious damage to his machine if he doesn't slam into a guardrail, the pilot who ground loops his airplane usually winds up parked on the propeller or a wing tip.

A ground loop usually begins when an airplane strikes the runway while drifting, either from a crosswind or from a sloppy approach. As the main gear slides sideways, the wing dips into the ground. Depending on how fast the airplane is traveling when it hit the ground, the skill of the pilot, the aircraft design and stability and the surface of the landing site, the airplane may just nick a wing or cartwheel on down the runway. Crosswinds probably account for 8 out of 10 ground loops because the pilot often has to dip one wing into the wind and touch down on one wheel. This is okay if you're lined up straight and paying attention to business. Wet grass, a slick or icy runway, or even a soft, sandy strip can make things get out of hand even quicker.

Failure of pilots in tri-gear airplanes to flare out soon enough and instead touch down on the nosewheel first is another cause of ground loops. When that nose gear hits first, you're suddenly driving a wheelbarrow that's instantly capable of going anywhere.

The Flight Safety Foundation tells us that some pilots use the wrong rudder in their attempt to control or correct a ground loop:

> Many an unhappy pilot has gone through the whirling dervish routine because in a moment of surprise, alarm or panic, he fed in the wrong rudder to correct the start of a ground loop. This stems from the fact that we are conditioned to using the rudder and aileron in the same direction while airborne. On the ground it's a different story. The rudder is used only for directional control, regardless of how the aileron is being used. Where the rub comes in is when the wing drops during ground roll, whether as the result of crosswind or the start of a turn. If the pilot is taken by surprise or isn't as sharp as he might be, he may react as he would in flight, i.e., opposite rudder and aileron to bring the wing up. When this happens it's all over except the accident report.

The greatest single factor in a ground loop is touching down while drifting. If the crosswind is too strong and you can't control your drift on final approach, go around and find another runway or another airport. If you start to flare out and that white center line goes wandering off to one side or another, hit that throttle and go around. The good pilot isn't the one who always makes a good landing, but rather the one who recognizes a bad one developing in time to abort it before getting into real trouble.

Too many pilots seem to think that once they're on

final approach they're committed to landing. Keep one hand on that throttle from the time you begin the base leg and don't hesitate to add power when and if it's necessary. It's often a temptation to clutch the control wheel with both hands for better control while landing in a stiff crosswind, but it's in just such a situation that you need one hand on the throttle more than ever.

It's much easier to ground loop on a sod or dirt airstrip than a paved runway. And on strips without a center line it's always harder to tell when the airplane is drifting.

So, how do you keep from making a ground loop? Pilot proficiency is the best answer. Practicing crosswind landings is good preventive medicine. Just as in any other landing, if the approach is good the touchdown and roll-out should be too. On a proper crosswind approach, you're already correcting for drift. If the wind is from the right, you can expect the wind to tend to lift the right wing at touchdown and the aircraft to weathervane to the right as the crosswind acts on the fin and rudder. If you've corrected properly for drift, you're already holding right aileron and left rudder at touchdown.

Using the throttle can help too. If the ground loop is to the right, adding power and torque may help some since it also applies a blast of slipstream to the rudder. But if you're already going to the left, it can make the situation worse.

Keep that airplane's nose *straight* before flare-out and touchdown. This may require any combination of dropping flaps, downwind rudder with upwind aileron and throttle. And if everything doesn't feel right and look okay, go around and try again.

Learning to be a pilot is more than just developing good aileron-rudder coordination. It's the process of becoming master of a very sophisticated machine—and this includes control of the airplane in bad situations as well as good ones. Flight training will provide the student with all the basic skills necessary to be a pilot, but it's up to the pilot to continue thinking about and practicing his art throughout his piloting career. The good pilot is the one who always considers himself a student regardless of how many hours he's logged.

11

Keeping
Fit
for
Flying

Flying is a new experience for many student pilots, and with it comes new and often strange sensations. Most of us adapt to new environments easily and quickly—as evidenced by the growing number of space flights and men's walks on the moon. Most of the experiences encountered in the air are pleasant. But not always. Some of us feel frightened or a little uneasy the first few times we go up. Still others suffer the miseries of airsickness. Both can be conquered.

Fear is perfectly normal and nothing to be ashamed of. You're in a foreign environment and feel more than a little helpless. You don't know the capability or reliability of this machine you're depending on, and it looks like a long, long way down if something goes wrong. Familiarity is the best cure for fear. As you begin to concentrate more and more on flying the airplane, your mind simply becomes crowded with too many things for fear to creep in again. And before long you'll begin to feel confident in both your piloting skill and in the airplane.

Airsickness, like seasickness or any other motion-induced disturbance, is primarily the result of the brain receiving conflicting and confusing messages from the eyes, organs of balance and muscle receptors. Thus, a person gets dizzy and feels nauseated, and because the stomach is so sensitive to nervous or mental fatigue, it reacts to these stimuli. The airlines have found that only about one percent or less of their passengers suffer from airsickness and that there are marked differences in sex and age. Adult men are the least susceptible. The incidence in women is five times as great as in men, and children are troubled nine times as often. Several factors enter into the cause of motion sickness, and one or all can play a part in any given individual. Up-and-down motion, like that experienced in rough or turbulent air, upsets the body's sensory system and can lead to nausea. Sometimes having a cold or other illness will increase the chances of getting airsick, because illness makes the body less able to withstand discomfort or unusual experiences of any kind.

Environment also contributes to the susceptibility of motion sickness. Many things can cause us to subconsciously tense up because we are uncomfortable or feel different. This feeling can then trigger a chain reaction that results in airsickness. One of the environmental factors affecting the body is temperature. Sometimes it gets excessively warm in light airplanes at low altitudes during summer months, and pretty cold in winter. Either may increase sensitivity to motion. Noise and vibration also can contribute to increased discomfort, fatigue and anxiety, particularly in people who are already apprehensive about flying.

The psychological factors associated with motion distress are difficult to define, but one of these, according to most experts, is fear. Anxiety over an upcoming flight or trip disturbs the nervous system and can lead to nausea that has no direct relationship to motion discomfort. Some people have a definite fear of becoming airsick and, sure enough, they talk themselves into it.

What can be done to minimize the problem? If a pilot should become ill and doesn't have a copilot, the safest thing is to land as soon as possible. But since motion sickness can always happen to pilots and passengers, it's important to know some of the things that can be done to avoid or relieve the causes and symptoms.

1. Look for distant landmarks and discuss their relative positions, distances and features. This minimizes concentration on nearby landmarks which may emphasize motion.

2. An explanation of the trip before takeoff and keeping passengers advised during the flight helps to reduce their apprehensions. Information concerning changes in direction, altitude, power

changes, engine noise, time en route and points of scenic interest tends to keep passengers from becoming bored and thinking about themselves. It also increases their understanding of what's going on and reduces anxiety.

3. Get some medication prior to the flight. Dramamine may be useful, especially for people who are susceptible to motion distress. The advice of a physician, preferably an aviation medical examiner, should be sought regarding dosage and desirability of the use of drugs in both adults and children.

4. Sit as near as possible to the center of gravity (usually near the wing), where there is less up-and-down or rocking motion.

5. Lie back if possible. This keeps the head reclined and increases the body tolerance to up-and-down motion.

6. Use earplugs to reduce noise.

7. Provide all the ventilation possible. This reduces cabin odors and keeps air fresh.

8. Fly at higher altitudes where the air is smoother. Flying at night may help too, since it reduces visual stimulation, and turbulence is usually less than during the day.

9. Avoid steep banks and sudden attitude changes. Gentle maneuvers will keep movement at a minimum and help passengers feel more comfortable.

10. Use oxygen at high altitudes. Oxygen may be useful when high altitudes are unavoidable. Of course, supplemental oxygen always should be available for passengers and pilots for flights above 10,000 feet.

DRUGS

Pilots are like everyone else—they get fatigued and may even be overweight and nervous. Dozens of drug prescriptions and medicines are available for each of these conditions, and many people think that most commonly used remedies are harmless and don't hinder our ability to perform routine daily tasks. But that isn't necessarily so. And pilots should know the pitfalls to some common medications.

Almost all drugs have side effects, and the severity of these effects is often increased by flying. Drowsiness, mental depression, decreased coordination, reduced sharpness of vision, diminished function of the organs of balance, increased nervousness, decreased depth perception and impaired judgment are all frequent side effects of many common medications. The FAA has strict regulations governing the use of drugs and alcohol, but the responsibility still lies with the pilot to exercise good judgment.

ASPIRIN—Most headache remedies contain aspirin, which is one of the few drugs normally accepted as having little or no adverse effect on people who are not allergic to it. However, many headache preparations contain pain relievers other than aspirin which reduce tolerance to altitude. Aspirin alone is considered safe for pilots.

NOSE DROPS AND INHALERS—In general, nose drops and inhalers cause little effect on the body other than the nose, if only used occasionally. Excessive use of either or both could lead to rapid heartbeat and increased nervousness, either of which may decrease the performance of the pilot.

ANTIHISTAMINES—Antihistamines are used for almost everything, including colds, motion sickness, allergies, hay fever and as sleeping pills. But they also may have dangerous side effects such as drowsiness, decreased coordination, mental depression, reduced sense of balance and diminished alertness. It's recommended that you not fly for 24 hours after taking even a usual dose of antihistamines.

COUGH MEDICINE—Cough medicines usually contain an ingredient which depresses the brain and cough center, a good-tasting syrup, an antihistamine and a decongestant. It also may decrease mental functions. The antihistamine decreases secretions and adds side effects. Decongestant side effects often cause increased heart rate and nervousness. In flight, all the side effects contribute to reduced pilot performance. Cold pills, which contain antihistamines, can also produce these same side effects.

TRANQUILIZERS—The pilot who is taking tranquilizers will react abnormally and poorly when under stress, such as when flying on instruments, in marginal weather, at night or in crowded traffic situations. A tranquilized pilot is a sluggish pilot. His alertness, judgment, reaction time and perception are all affected adversely. The FAA recommends that pilots not fly within a 24-hour period after taking tranquilizers. Stomach soothers, heartburn preparations and ulcer medications also have a depressant or tranquilizing ingredient—so the same rule applies to them also.

PEP PILLS—Pep pills are an artificial and harmful means of increasing energy and fighting fatigue. Pep pills may cause blurred vision, nervousness, irritability, impaired judgment and loss of coordination. Reducing pills are essentially pep pills with sedatives or tranquilizers and should be avoided by pilots.

MOTION-SICKNESS DRUGS—While useful for passengers, motion-sickness drugs should not be used by pilots unless prescribed for a student who experience airsickness early in flight training. In this case, he should have a qualified instructor at the dual controls, and the entire operation should be under the guidance of a physician and with the knowledge and consent of the instructor. Motion-sickness drugs are basically antihistamines, which have already been discussed.

ALCOHOL

The effects of alcohol are similar to those of tranquilizers and sleeping pills, and alcohol may continue circulating in the blood for several hours—especially if you don't eat anything after downing that martini. Federal Aviation Regulations require pilots to wait eight hours after drinking any alcoholic beverage before flying an airplane. But common sense should tell you to wait even longer if you've put away more than one or two drinks. Alcohol can remain in the bloodstream for 24 hours or more, and although you may not actually feel its effects, your perception and reaction time can be dulled considerably. A good rule is to allow 24 hours between the last drink and takeoff time.

Medical research has substantiated the following physiological and psychological effects of alcohol:

1. A dulling of critical judgment.
2. A decreased sense of responsibility.
3. Diminished skill reactions and coordination.
4. Decreased speed and strength of muscular reflexes (even after one ounce of alcohol).
5. Efficiency of eye movements decreased 20 percent during reading (after one ounce of alcohol).
6. Significantly increased frequency of errors (after one ounce).
7. Constriction of visual field.
8. Decreased ability to see under dim light.
9. Loss of efficiency of sense of touch.
10. Decreased memory and reasoning ability.
11. Increased susceptibility to fatigue and decreased attention span.
12. Decreased relevance of responses in free-association test, with an increase in nonsensical reactions.
13. Increased self-confidence with decreased insight into immediate capabilities and mental and physical status.

CARBON MONOXIDE

The cabin compartment of most single-engine airplanes is heated by air circulating over exhaust manifolds. Flying with a defective heater could be dangerous, just as driving a car with a leaky muffler is risky. Carbon monoxide is a colorless, odorless, tasteless gas always present in exhaust fumes. For biochemical reasons, carbon monoxide has a greater affinity for the hemoglobin of the blood than oxygen. Once carbon monoxide is absorbed in the blood, it sticks to the hemoglobin and actually blocks the normal mixture of oxygen with the hemoglobin.

The beginning of carbon monoxide poisoning produces blurred thinking and dizziness, sometimes accompanied by a headache and upset stomach. If carbon monoxide is suspected, cabin heat should be turned off immediately and a window or the ventilation system opened. If the airplane is equipped with oxygen masks, oxygen can help relieve the symptoms, but the carbon monoxide may remain in the bloodstream for up to 48 hours. For that reason, and because the fumes will probably continue to leak into the passenger compartment, the pilot should land as soon as possible and have the trouble corrected before resuming the flight. A good prevention for this hazard is an inexpensive carbon-monoxide detector for the cabin.

ANESTHETICS

It's a good idea to wait at least 48 hours after either a local or general anesthetic before piloting an airplane. Although the major effects of such anesthetics may appear to wear off within a few hours, they can continue to interfere with normal coordination, judgment and reaction time for much longer. If in doubt about the right time to resume flying, check with your doctors or flight examiner.

BLOOD DONATIONS

Giving blood may well be a noble gesture—but it isn't compatible with flying. Blood circulation following a donation takes several weeks to return to normal and, although effects are slight at ground level, there are risks when flying during this period. The FAA recommends pilots not to volunteer as blood donors if they plan on flying within the next several days.

HYPOXIA

One common hazard all pilots should be alert to is hypoxia, which is the medical term for an insufficient supply of oxygen to the body. When hypoxia strikes, the pilot and passengers experience an increased breathing rate, lightheaded or dizzy sensation, tingling or warm sensation, sweating, reduced visual field, sleepiness and a blue coloring of skin, fingernails and lips.

Subtle hypoxia can begin at only 5000 feet at night. In most people, night vision will be blurred and narrowed. At 8000 feet, night vision is reduced as much as 25 percent without supplemental oxygen. Little or no effects will be noticed during daylight at these altitudes. At 10,000 feet there is only slight oxygen deficiency, and pilots flying at that altitude for short periods of time during the day won't notice any change. However, anyone flying at that altitude for more than four hours will begin to notice difficulty in concentrating, reasoning, solving problems and making precise adjustments of the airplane's controls. It's a spooky feeling, and a dangerous situation. At 15,000 feet, drowsiness, a headache, weariness, fatigue and a false sense of well-being will begin within two hours. Proceeding up to 20,000 feet, where the oxygen supply is less than half that at sea level, complete collapse and convulsions will occur within 15 minutes.

Probably the most dangerous aspect of hypoxia is its gradual and insidious onset. Its production of a false feeling of well-being, called euphoria, is especially dangerous since it obscures a person's ability to realize what is actually happening to him. The person lapsing into hypoxia commonly believes things are getting progressively better as he nears total collapse. Because it affects the central nervous system, the general effects of hypoxia are, in many respects, very similar to alcoholic intoxication. An individual suffering from hypoxia will behave much the same as someone who has consumed five or six ounces of whiskey.

Recovery from hypoxia is quick, usually within 15 seconds after oxygen is administered. But transient dizziness may occur for some time afterward, and the severely affected individual often will be quite fatigued for several hours.

Susceptibility to hypoxia varies, and there are some people who can tolerate altitudes well above 10,000 feet without any significant effects. It's equally true that there are individuals who suffer from hypoxia below 10,000 feet. As a general rule, individuals who do not exercise regularly or who are not in good physical condition will have less resistance to oxygen deficiency.

Also, if you've overindulged in alcohol, are a moderate to heavy smoker, or take certain kinds of medication as already mentioned, you're more likely to be susceptible to hypoxia. Susceptibility can also vary in the same individual from day to day, or even from morning to evening.

The best prevention is to either avoid flight at those altitudes where hypoxia is likely to occur or to make sure the oxygen system (if the airplane is so equipped) is working properly. Federal Aviation Regulations require the use of supplemental oxygen while flying above 12,500 feet for more than 30 minutes. Above 14,000 feet, supplemental oxygen should be used continuously.

VERTIGO

In our day-by-day lives the body receives hundreds of "messages" that our sensory system must interpret immediately for us to respond to. Although our nervous system is very complex, we rely basically on information gathered by the eyes, nerve endings in the muscles and about the joints (commonly called "seat-of-the-pants" sensation) and certain tiny balance organs which are part of the inner ear. The ability to orient ourselves correctly in relation to our environment, and then to respond accordingly, is fundamental to survival. The same is true, of course, when piloting an airplane. However, pilots can run into certain conditions where sensory perception fails or gives false information.

A pilot who has flown into clouds and can no longer

use ground references will literally not be able to tell which end is up. The brain struggles to decipher signals sent from the senses, but without the clue normally supplied by vision, incorrect or conflicting interpretations may result. The product of such sensory confusion is a dizzy, whirling sensation called *vertigo*, or *spacial disorientation*. For example, a pilot flying at night above an inclined cloud bank well-illuminated by moonlight might suffer sensory confusion. He might assume a cloud layer to be flat, or parallel to the ground, and align the airplane with the cloud bank, which would put the airplane in a roll and cause either an increase or decrease in altitude. This is why you learn to fly blind under the hood during training for the private license—but it is still hazardous to fly in clouds without extensive instrument training and in an airplane not equipped for instrument flight. And it's surprising how difficult it is sometimes to believe in those instruments when your sensory system feeds you conflicting information.

Another common problem associated with night flying is confusing ground lights with the stars. Incidents are recorded by the FAA where a pilot literally flew into the ground because he thought lights of a city on the horizon were actually stars.

There are other causes of vertigo in addition to sensory confusion. *Flicker vertigo*, caused by a steadily blinking light, results in dizziness, nausea, unconsciousness or even severe reactions similar to an epileptic fit. In a single-engine airplane flying toward the sun, the propeller can sometimes cause a flicker-vertigo effect, especially when the engine is throttled back for a landing approach. If you can't otherwise avoid this situation on a landing approach, the best thing to do is give the engine a shot of power once or twice to break the constant rhythm.

Aside from all the various medical and biological factors just discussed, one of the major considerations for staying fit is your mental attitude. A pilot is continually required to evaluate information, perform complex tasks and make quick decisions. If you're under stress—because of work, financial or family problems—you're not in the best health for flying an airplane. Flying can be relaxing for those who enjoy it, but piloting an airplane is always demanding even under ideal conditions.

Stress and anxiety are two health problems that can easily get a pilot into trouble. When we're disturbed or upset by something, we don't cope with emergencies very well. If a pilot flying in this state of mind runs into bad weather, or if he gets temporarily lost or disoriented, he could panic and compound the problem.

We all have our bad days—try to pick the good ones for flying.

12
Who
Flies
What
and
Why

Maybe you've been thinking: "Gee, I'd love to learn to fly, but what good would it do me? I mean—it's awfully expensive and a lot of work just to be able to take friends up for a ride once in a while on a Sunday afternoon."

If that's what's bothering you, then let's explore flying a little more, as well as some of the men and women involved. Once you earn that private ticket, a whole new world of fun, travel, adventure, sport, business advantages and quite possibly even a new career open up to you.

Let's start with business. Maybe your impression of business flying goes something like this:

A small, sleek jet rolls up to the terminal and is met there by a long black limousine. A troupe of well-dressed executive types climb out of the car and, carrying their expensive leather attaché cases, glance at their wristwatches and climb into the jet. The door closes behind them, and in a minute the airplane goes zipping off into the wild blue yonder.

Glamorous, yes. But hardly typical. If you spend any time at your local airport, you're much more likely to see a taxicab delivering a salesman to his single-engine Piper Cherokee, or a VW bus pull up next to a medium-sized twin-engine airplane and a team of specialists board it for a trouble-shooting trip to some distant factory. Or maybe a surgeon might taxi up in his Beechcraft Bonanza and be met by a colleague who needs assistance on a delicate operation.

This is all business flying, and almost every type of airplane—including those used at flight schools—is adaptable to business missions. And the idea is growing every day. The jets and turboprops (jet engines that drive propellers) account for a relatively small percentage of the airplanes used for business. To justify owning a jet or a turboprop, a company must have considerable financial ability, plus the need for contacts over a large area. But if all these needs are met, a jet is a major asset to any company—large or small. Most companies use their jets and turboprops for a lot more than flying the top men to important meetings. Some virtually run a private airline that continually flies between cities where company facilities are located. Others use fleets of airplanes to shuttle customers from their home bases to company headquarters. It's an effective and efficient way of doing business for those who can afford it. But not many companies can.

Other businesses want *nearly* everything offered by the super-fast jets and turboprop jobs, and this need has led to a proliferation of twin-engine pressurized models powered by piston engines that cruise along at around 250 mph.

But by far the most numerous business airplanes of all are the small twin-engine and single-engine craft. Where most of the jets, turboprops and pressurized airplanes are flown by professional pilots, most flying businessman usually pilot their own twin or single. This is probably the most important kind of flying to you, and if you have business use for an airplane, this is where you will begin.

But you may figure a businessman can use the airlines just as easily and inexpensively as a private airplane.

Not really. Most scheduled airlines offer good service to major cities and metropolitan areas. But smaller towns across the country are often bypassed altogether. The key to success for scheduled air carriers is in filling seats in big airplanes. The airlines now do about 70 percent of their business in only 22 cities, and a town or city that offers only a handful of people a day as potential passengers just can't be served without disastrous financial results.

A businessman who needs to travel to Yucca Valley,

This vintage Piper Cub trainer has been meticulously restored to look like a World War II trainer. Notice the extended window panels aft of the rear seat.

California, or Terre Haute, Indiana, will find little help among commercial airlines. Even when traveling between two medium-sized cities, the business traveler —particularly when following a tight schedule—is often frustrated by a lack of timely airline flights. Making a 10 A.M. meeting might mean having to fly in the day before. And if the meeting runs into the late afternoon, the last flight out might have already left, meaning another night in a hotel and more valuable time lost.

The flexibility of business flying helps companies diversify, too. Many have found it possible to locate a plant in a smallish town that really wants and needs industry—if that town has an airport.

Here's what businessman-pilot Richard L. Collins says about traveling in his own airplane:

"Of all the things the airplane does for me, I think its ability to keep trips down to one-day jaunts and to allow me to leave right after the conclusion of business are the most valuable.

"I live in the middle of the country, and move around over all of it, east and west, for a total of about 75,000 miles a year of business travel. I do it all in a Cherokee Six, a pregnant version of the Cherokee trainer. I used the airlines only once last year, and can honestly say that that trip was the only time I felt that airline travel offered a clear-cut advantage over my private plane.

"Last year, I was home 34 nights that would have been spent on the road if my traveling had been done by any means other than my little business airplane. When you travel a lot, it means much to be able to swap a night in a motel for a night at home. And the airplane helps efficiency too, because being tied to someone else's schedule when making business calls can be frustrating, to say the least."

And the fun of flying, Collins quickly admits, is an added asset. Collins says that on longer trips from major cities, his 160-mph airplane can often outpace the jet airliners. How? The advantage comes in being able to leave as soon as business is finished.

"The other day," Collins said, in citing an example, "I was in Washington, D.C., for a meeting that ended early, just before noon. I went on to the airport and headed westward. There was a strong wind, and I wondered if this might not be one of those trips that would have best been done on the airline. I checked when I

got home, though, and found that my little airplane
had taken me home halfway across the country an hour
quicker than the best available airline schedule."

This doesn't mean anyone is knocking the airlines
with such comparisons. They provide one of the finest
transportation systems in the world, and their safety
record is magnificent. But they still don't have all the
answers to many business-travel needs. Business flying
is a big part of general aviation, and it's still growing.
There is no way to list all the things that business flying touches, and helps, in the country, but without it,
a lot of companies and individuals would be sorely
handicapped. And perhaps a great many communities,
too.

But perhaps you're thinking about a flying career.

The general aviation industry encompasses all manner of civil aircraft from two-place Piper Cubs to flying
hotels like the Boeing 747s. And airplanes are used in
hundreds of ways. It would probably be easier to list

*This classic AT-6 fighter of World War II fame is now pop-
ular as a racing and aerobatic airplane.*

the jobs they *don't* do. The small airplane, popularly thought to be a pleasure craft of the wealthy, has proved itself a reliable workhorse in pipeline and power-line patrol, aerial surveying and photography, freighting, charters and air-taxi flying, crop spraying and dusting, border patrol, ambulance service, advertising, sightseeing, corporate flying—the list is endless, with new roles discovered each year. A sizable number of pilots are kept busy ferrying new ships to owners here and overseas. Anyone who imagines that small Cessnas, Beeches and Pipers are weekend toys has never been to Alaska, where airplanes and pilots outnumber cars and drivers and where many frontier points are linked by air and by air alone. This end of aviation gets little publicity. It may not be worth the attention of magazine writers, but it's certainly worth the attention of young pilots eager to broaden their experience and build hours.

The pilot with a commercial license can find flying work if he goes to where it's happening. His first job or his fourth may not be the answer he seeks, but they will be steps up the ladder to better things. The bigger and faster the airplane, the more experience is required. Companies that invest from $50,000 to a million dollars or more in an airplane are choosy about who flies it. They interview few applicants with less than 1500 hours and an airline transport rating, and some of this time had best be in high-performance types. A college degree is an advantage and increasingly a necessity in corporate flying, as pilots are often expected to involve themselves with management work when not flying. The requirements and rewards of this demanding

Spot-landing contests at fly-ins are popular fun with pilots of all levels of experience.

branch of piloting vary with the companies that operate executive ships and can be rated from fair to excellent. The best idea is to make your own investigation of all employment possibilities.

A lot has been written and passed around about the good deal airline pilots have. Too much, in fact. The pay, working conditions, equipment, security, fringe benefits and way of life are described in such glowing terms that it makes any other flying job seem second best.

The young pilot starting out on a career in flying should know more about these glamorous airmen. Airline pilots are subject to pressures, restraints, surveillance and regimentation to an extent rarely appreciated outside their ranks. Every mile they travel from gate to gate is directed and monitored and every minute of it recorded by equipment in the ships. Every word said in the cockpit is likewise recorded by shipboard equipment. All radio contacts are recorded on the ground. Twice a year (once for copilots and engi-

Skimming in over the trees on a spot-landing try.

neers) a captain must pass a federally supervised physical, then prove to the satisfaction of his company and government that he's just as sharp as he was six months ago. This means ground school, written and oral exams, flight checks.

During routine line flying, a company or federal agent may take the extra cockpit seat to observe, without prior warning.

An airline pilot must continuously cater to the whims and demands of a score of outside groups, each of which wants something different. His passengers want a smooth ride and an on-time arrival. The company needs a profitable operation. Residents near the airport demand less noise. The FAA expects strict compliance with the law. City officials ask him to land his DC-10 on a runway built for DC-6s. He can't do it all, so he satisfies himself first, doing what he thinks is best and safest, and then spreads what's left as evenly as possible. It usually works. But when it doesn't, and he's called into the office to explain, he is likely to find himself a guilty man trying to prove his innocence.

As for security, the airline pilot carries expensive disability coverage, knowing that for every captain who makes it to age 60, three others will drop out along the way, some with physical problems that wouldn't prevent any other professional from completing a productive career.

Nor is airline flying the right job for the individual bent on doing his own thing in his own way.

Yet, for all its rigid and difficult framework, few airline pilots would trade work with other pilots, fewer still would swap their job for more secure ground duties—even at the same pay.

The airlines hire the best men they can find and rarely have to accept less than two years of college, 1000 hours of flying and a commercial license with instrument rating. Many trunk lines now require a flight-engineer rating in turboprops, a slip of paper worth about $4000, if you buy the training. Qualified veterans can sidestep most of this expense by attending a Veterans Administration–approved school and can pick up other ratings the same way.

But what about the young person sold on a career in flying? How do you get started? The first step is to learn everything you can about it—*all of it.* Resist the urge to focus attention on one branch of this broad and complex industry until you have a fair grasp of the entire scene. The time to specialize will come later. Even years of waiting, of thinking and learning about an aviation career while completing your formal education, can be and should be as important and useful to your overall plans as the training you'll receive in the cockpit. Competition for jobs in aviation is keen, and all the education you can get will help.

Getting started, of course, is the first step. Boiled down, a pilot is a technician who must solve the same riddle every time he goes to work. It's the ageless riddle of thrust and drag, lift and gravity, and it applies equally to a Piper Cherokee or a Boeing 747. Once he has mastered it in a simple trainer, he advances to faster, heavier equipment as rapidly as his ability and ambition allow. And for as long as the money lasts. Flight training is not cheap. But if it leads to a flying career, it's not expensive either. Like a doctor, a pilot can earn far above average pay once he has the right tickets in his pocket and the right experience behind him. But someone has to pay the bills en route.

You might consider letting us taxpayers pay the bill.

The Veterans Administration will pick up 90 percent of the tab for advanced training leading to a commercial license. If you haven't already been in the service, you might also give that some thought as a way of getting your flight training. The Army, Navy and Air Force were the launching grounds for many pilots now enjoying civilian flying careers. This might be a good

This pusher-type homebuilt was converted from a glider.

road for you. A college degree and excellent health are the current requirements for the Air Force and Navy, while the Army will talk seriously with you if you have 60 hours of college credits, and even less in some cases. There is a catch, however. The military is not in the business of training pilots for civilian careers. In exchange for flight training, you must serve a tour of active duty, the length of which depends on the terms of your enlistment. But if you enter the service immediately after finishing college, you can train, fulfill your obligation and return to civilian life still young enough to qualify for a good position. And the airlines and operators of high-performance business airplanes give preference to pilots who have gained valuable experience, proved their abilities and logged considerable hours in military aircraft.

A good many military pilots elect to remain in the service until retirement. There's a lot to be said for such a career—the benefits are excellent and you'll never find a better opportunity to fly a large variety of aircraft. Until recently, military flight training was a road open only to men. But in 1973, Lt. (jg) Barbara Allen became the first woman to graduate from the Navy's rigorous and demanding flight school in Corpus Christi, Texas. And although federal law prohibits women from flying jet fighters or bombers (the Equal Rights Amendment would change that), she still will gain valuable experience flying multiengine transports.

If you had the money, you could buy enough training and solid experience to qualify for any flying job, assuming you also have the excellent health, ability and tremendous personal drive that go with it. You could log 1000 hours and along the way earn all the ratings any employer would want. But for the same amount of money you could put yourself through an expensive private university two or three times. Obviously, this isn't the way to do it. People with that sort of money buy and fly their own airplanes and aren't interested in piloting as a career.

Appropriately named "Breezy," this homemade job is strictly a fair-weather airplane!

The average person goes to an approved school and buys a flying course that includes ground and flight training. They emerge with more than 40 hours in their logbook and a private pilot's license in their wallet or purse—which is by now roughly $800 to $1000 lighter. This rating will allow them to fly a light plane, make cross-country trips, so long as they avoid bad weather, and haul passengers, providing they aren't charged for the ride. This is the point where most students make up their mind about flying. After this first brush they either elect to keep advancing, continue on a limited basis as a hobby or drop it altogether.

If you like what you see, the next step will be the commercial ticket. Costs vary with location, equipment and so forth, but $2500 is a fairly accurate figure for earning a commercial rating. Another $600 or so will pay for winning the instructor's license. Now the door is open for you to earn money with this new talent by carrying passengers for hire and teaching others to fly. If you can find a job.

There's no shortage of pilots with these credentials who have 200 or 300 hours of flying time. And unless you know somebody, or hit it very lucky, it isn't going to be easy to find work. But any enterprising youngster can always find ways to build time at no expense to himself and even clear a few dollars in the process. The more time you log, the more employable you become. You're also on the inside now, meeting the professionals, learning about the best flying jobs and what it takes to get them.

At this point, a student pilot has invested roughly

$4000 in starting a flying career. And if that sounds like a staggering, impossible sum, don't lose heart. Aviation is long on hard, menial chores and short on people willing to get their hands dirty. It's always been this way, and there have always been young people keen enough to cash in on it.

"In five more years," quipped one executive pilot with more than 10,000 hours in his logbook, "I will have logged an hour of flying for every airplane I washed when I was in high school."

In fact, the same qualities necessary to get a student through flight training and win the ratings and experience—resourcefulness and determination—are the same ones necessary to make it as a top professional pilot.

Because of the awkward generic nature of our language, it's clumsy to say "he or she" when "he" can mean both sexes. To replace the masculine pronoun with "one" just sounds too stilted for me. The point is, women are hardly to be excluded from flying or any discussion of it. Women today—both young and old—play an increasingly important role in aviation. Maybe Lt. Barbara Allen is the exception, but she *is* a good example of the growing opportunities open to women in all areas of aviation. And although women still may be a rare sight in the cockpit of a military aircraft or commercial airliner, they are hardly strangers to flying.

There are women on the flight line every day, preflight checking their airplanes, filing flight plans, talking to the control tower, executing instrument landing approaches. They are teaching new students, both male and female, to fly. They are reporting highway traffic from helicopters and taking aerial photos, or carrying medicine, film, executives and tourists. Women are practicing for air races and giving in-laws spectacular tours of the metropolitan area or countryside. They make cross-country flights or just get off by themselves for a little solitude.

Women use airplanes to get themselves to golf tournaments, tennis matches, rodeos, swimming meets and ski resorts. There are women race pilots who enter several national events every year. These races are proficiency contests, carefully regulated according to international rules, and requiring sound knowledge and superb piloting skill. Other women prefer aerobatic flying, with its special aircraft, swinging maneuvers and keen international competition.

Some women fly because their men do. Rather than be passive cargo or adoring idolators, they get into the act themselves. And this doesn't dampen mutual respect and esteem—it enhances it. Intelligent sharing always builds a better relationship. And it's more fun. No little girl today should discount flying as a possible career. There are already countless possibilities, and the opportunities are increasing every day.

Even advanced age won't count you out if you feel and think young. Marion Rice Hart recently flew from Washington, D.C., to Ceylon and back. She made the trip alone, piloting and navigating her single-engine Beechcraft Bonanza.

Mrs. Hart is 82 years old.

She didn't take her first lesson until she was 54. She would have started younger, but "in those days all you

Flour-sack-bombing contests are a popular test of piloting skills.

could do was go up and come down," she says. "You couldn't go anywhere." And Marion definitely wanted to go somewhere.

She has flown across the Atlantic Ocean seven times in the last 20 years; four of those trips were solo. Mrs. Hart figures she flew 35,000 miles on the Ceylon trip—the equivalent of one and a half times around the world.

She has flown across the Atlantic Ocean seven times with a copilot directly from Gander to Shannon. That trip then took her as far as India and Thailand. For the next nine years she was content with the Western Hemisphere. She flew around South America "and all those islands," but in 1962, with a new and more powerful Bonanza (260 horsepower instead of 180) she set out for the Old World again. Since then she has crossed the ocean roughly every other year.

In 1966, at the age of 74, she made her first solo crossing. When she seeks directions to the weather office or some airport facility, she is often asked, "Where is your captain?" or "Who is your companion?"

Although Mrs. Hart has been around the world in a sailboat, she says she will never attempt such a feat in a plane. "The Pacific is too big," she says. "It would take something like 16 hours, and that's too much. And I don't have to do it—I don't have to make records."

But Mrs. Hart's passion for flying is primarily an outgrowth of her lifelong wanderlust.

"I never did anything really well enough to be a professional," she says. "I never really wanted to, either. It sounds very exciting to be a professional pilot on an airliner, but all you do is go back and forth. If you want to stop over you can't."

And Marion Hart doesn't like being that tied down.

Flying has always seemed exciting and more than a little daring to the general public. The image has always been encouraged by Hollywood film makers—along with a few colorful pilots willing to crash airplanes for a living. Guys like Charlie Stoffer.

If you call 79-year-old Charlie an "old buzzard," he won't give you a cranky frown. More than likely you'll see a proud grin. That's because Charlie—more formally known as Col. Charles Stoffer, U.S. Air Force, retired—truly is an old Buzzard, last surviving member of the once famous Buzzard Squadron of daredevil Hollywood stunt fliers who thrilled millions of moviegoers in the late 1920s. Charlie is also one of the last of the old-time Jenny biplane barnstormers, one of the last fly-by-the-seat-of-your-pants, goggle-wearing, Smilin' Jack aviators.

These days he putters around in the garden of his home in Greenbrae, an upper-middle-class suburb of San Francisco, instead of putting around in aeroplanes (that's what they called them when Charlie started flying back in 1917).

But his memories of those glory days remain as sharp and clear as a young eagle's eyes.

Stoffer seems most proud of his days with the Buzzards. That group, also known as the "Squadron of Death," was formed by the greatest of all the old-time Hollywood stunt pilots, Dick Grace, to dogfight and, occasionally, to crash airplanes in front of the cameras. It was as a substitute for Grace, who had been injured in an earlier crack-up, that Stoffer performed one of the most spectacular crashes in movie history—deliberately flying an old biplane between two trees set 12 feet apart.

The crash ripped the wings off the plane. Stoffer came through shaken but unscathed—he thought. "But just last month I had some X rays of my chest, and the doctor told me I had had several ribs broken," Stoffer said. That was in May 1973, some 45 years after the crash, in which he apparently broke them and didn't realize it.

Stoffer did one other crash in *Lilac Time,* which starred Colleen Moore and Gary Cooper. "For the tree crash," Stoffer remembers, "I got paid $2500. I only got $1500 for the other one—the easy one."

Charlie shrugs off the danger of controlled crashes. "You glide in very slowly," he says. "It's really like an auto crash at 20 to 30 miles an hour. It looks more sensational than it really is."

Stunt flying is still alive and thriving across the country. Only today it's called "aerobatics" and comes in the form of super-sophisticated sport flying and competition. And it's come a long way from the days of the stunting barnstormer. About the only similarity is that sometimes the airplanes are flown upside down.

The first chapter of the International Aerobatic

World War II trainers, like this vintage Beechcraft T-34, make popular sport-flying airplanes.

Club (IAC) was organized in February 1970 as a division of the Experimental Aircraft Association to serve those with an avid interest in aerobatics. Since then the group has grown to some 30 chapters across the country.

Aerobatics provides goals that any pilot can work toward in a closely monitored, tightly controlled situation, with safety considerations receiving top priority. The club has established five categories of achievement awards that can be earned by pilot members which require a gradual increase in proficiency in order to successfully complete all maneuvers in each respective category.

Starting with loops, spins and rolls, a pilot can progress through the Basic category on to Sportman, Intermediate, Advanced and, finally, to the Unlimited category. Each category has a set of maneuvers that must be mastered. It's strictly up to each pilot whether he wants to compete against fellow IAC members in any of these categories at any of a growing number of aerobatic contests held each year. And when it comes to contests, the IAC enforces some strict rules for the safety of both pilots and spectators.

Aerobatic pilots are judged not only on how well they perform their maneuvers, but if they are accomplished within a specified time limit and within the confines of a precisely defined block of airspace, called the *framing area*, and on *rhythm*, which is the timing between maneuvers. Definite altitude minimums are part of the framing areas, and if a contestant drops below that limit he will be disqualified.

This beautiful little homemade Pitts Special is piloted by 21-year-old Ken Cantrell, picked by many experts to be one of the four or five top aerobatic pilots in the world within the next four or five years.

The lure of aerobatics draws pilots with highly varied background and levels of experience, both as active contest participants and as officials working on the ground. It gives the newly licensed private pilot an opportunity to meet and work with the seasoned airline captain on grounds where they share a mutual interest. Like the highly skilled race-car driver, the aerobatic pilot perfects his skills to a point that allows him to squeeze the maximum performance from his machine —and extend his abilities beyond what most other pilots can even imagine.

But if aerobatics sound a little too demanding, but the lure of competition still draws you, there are plenty of other opportunities for weekend fun and a chance

to polish your flying skills. Various flying clubs and organizations are always conducting "fly-ins" that offer
spot-landing contests and flour-sack bombing competition, along with colorful displays of home-built and
restored aircraft. The mood at these gatherings is always festive and friendly. But then, when you get a
bunch of pilots and airplanes together, it always is.

If you're seriously contemplating learning to fly,
don't let the expense stop you. Everything costs a lot
these days, from football tickets to nail polish. And
what do you buy with these? Fleeting pleasure that
vanishes in a month or even an instant. But flying
money buys you a style of life, renovates rusty brains,
moves muscles out of storage and sharpens the senses.
In short, it's a good investment for the person who pre-
fers to get out and do things rather than watching
someone else have all the fun.

APPENDIX ONE
Becoming a Pilot

Basic Requirements. One of the first requirements for learning to fly is physical fitness. To find out if you qualify, your flying school will require you to pass a physical examination given by an FAA-certified doctor. Upon passing this exam you will be given a third-class medical certificate, which will serve as your student pilot license. When your instructor endorses it, this certificate will be your license to solo. If your medical certificate expires, you can no longer legally exercise your privilege as a private pilot.

The second-class medical certificate is required of commercial pilots, and the first-class ticket for airline-transport-rated pilots. A brief comparison of the physical requirements follows, so that you may see the differences. You may, if you wish, obtain a medical certificate for a higher rating than you hold, and many pilots do so as a means of maintaining and demonstrating good general health.

Third class

Valid 24 calendar months after month of issue.

Eyes correctable to 20/30 in each eye; red, green, white color discrimination.

Ears, nose, throat, equilibrium and nervous system within normal limits.

No history of heart disease or other cardiovascular problems.

Good general health.

No history of diabetes requiring drugs for control, alcoholism, epilepsy, drug addiction or psychotic behavior.

Second class

Valid 12 calendar months after month of issue.

Eyes 20/100 or better, correctable to 20/20 in each eye; red, green, white color discrimination, normal field of vision.

Ears, nose, throat, equilibrium and nervous system within normal limits.

No history of heart disease or other cardiovascular problems.

Good general health.

No history of diabetes requiring drugs for control, alcoholism, epilepsy, drug addiction or psychotic behavior.

First class

Valid 6 calendar months after month of issue.

Eyes 20/100 or better, correctable to 20/20 in each eye, no color blindness, normal field of vision.

Ears, nose, throat, equilibrium and nervous system within normal limits.

No history of heart disease or other cardiovascular problems; annual EKG required after age 35.

Good general health.

No history of diabetes requiring drugs for control, alcoholism, epilepsy, drug addiction or psychotic behavior.

WAIVERS AND EXEMPTIONS

The FAA has special procedures for persons who may not be able, for one reason or another, to pass their medical examinations. The most common problems which are waivered in FAA medicals are visual defects. But there are several others where either a waiver or an exemption may be obtained. The loss of a limb, for example, may be exempted, through a medical flight test—during which a pilot must prove competence consistent with air safety.

Even some seemingly impossible cases such as diabetes or coronary disease can be handled by the granting of special time-limited medical certificates. Where a diabetic has satisfactorily achieved a stabilized condition through diet, for example, the FAA might grant a certificate good for six months. If you have any doubts or questions, a check with your regional flight surgeon's office at the FAA might be helpful.

Private License

Student

You must be at least 16 years old.

You must have:

a command of the English language.

a third-class medical certificate.

a Federal Communications Commission radio operator's permit.

Solo

Your medical certificate must be signed by a certified flight instructor for the type of airplane you are flying.

Private

You must be at least 17 years old when you take the FAA flight check, and your medical certificate must be current at that time.

Your instructor must be satisfied that you understand the necessary operating rules and limitations in the Federal Aviation Regulations.

You must have passed the FAA private-pilot written examination with a score of 70 or better. You must have an understanding of, and be able to answer, questions about:

the FARs applicable to the private pilot
the National Transportation Safety Board's regulations
the *Airman's Information Manual*
basic meteorology

for the oral exam given at the time of the flight check. You must be proficient in preflight, starting and running up the engine, takeoffs and landings, traffic-pattern procedures, basic flight control, straight and level flight, climbing and gliding turns, stalls and recoveries and various emergency procedures.

You must have had a minimum of 40 hours of flight time, broken down into:

20 hours of dual instruction signed by a certified flight instructor, including:
three hours cross-country (a trip with a landing at least 25 miles from the home base);

three hours night flying with a minimum of
10 takeoffs and landings;
three hours of dual review, signed by your
CFI, before the flight check.
20 hours of solo flight, including:
10 cross-country trips with landings at least 50
miles from the home base, and one trip
with three landings, each 100 miles apart;
three takeoffs and landings made at a controlled field.

The flight check will include:

the maneuvers required for solo plus advanced
stalling maneuvers, turns about a point and
special landings and takeoffs;
navigation by charts, compass and radio aids;
flight with sole reference to instruments.

APPENDIX TWO
Choosing a School

Once you have made up your mind that you want to learn to fly, the next step will be selecting a school. If there is only one airport where you live, with one firm offering instruction, your choice will be easy. In most cases, however, you'll have several schools to choose from and may well wonder how to be a wise shopper.

It's fairly safe to say that any FAA-approved flight school is going to give you competent expert instruction. Prices are generally similar, too, so your decision will most likely be made on word-of-mouth recommendation, the atmosphere you find, the attractiveness of the facilities and the kind of airplane you want to fly.

Very often, a potential student lives in an area where he or she can choose between small, uncontrolled airports or large commercial ones. Chances are good that the smaller field will charge lower rates than the firm operating out of a larger facility, and the atmosphere at the smaller operation is likely to be much friendlier and more casual. On the other hand, the municipal field, with its higher prices, may have a more professional attitude, be more efficient and have both a fully staffed mechanical shop and a sizable line of airplanes on hand, so that a trainer is usually available. All these advantages, however, can raise the cost of your instruction considerably.

The average cost for renting a trainer will be somewhere between $17 and $20 an hour. The instructor's fee will be about $7 to $12 an hour, bringing the total cost of an hour of dual instruction to between $24 and $32. The FAA requires a minimum of 40 hours of instruction and training, bringing the cost to approximately $950 to $1300. The national average for students, however, is actually 63 hours of training time. This means you can expect the cost to be closer to $1500 to $2000 for earning a private pilot's license.

Cost can be reduced under a variety of plans. If, for example, you make a deposit on account of various amounts, you may be given a percentage credit or discount. Many of the larger schools make arrangements with local banks, and some even offer training and aircraft rental through credit cards.

But even with all the options available to them, many student pilots choose to pay as they go, on an hour-by-hour basis. Although this can be more expensive, they find that the initial outlay of $1000 or more is simply too much of a financial burden. Some choose to buy a block of instruction for a week—perhaps two or more hours. This regular payment of $40 to $50 is sometimes less painful than borrowing the money or dipping heavily into the savings.

Most schools—especially the larger ones—have a variety of payment plans and will work with you to find a way of working out something that fits your resources.

Many of the larger flight schools around the country are affiliated with airplane manufacturers. Several of the manufacturers have developed their own individual training programs, designed to help the student learn about flying and reduce the time and money he must spend. If you enroll in such a program, you will be sold a kit that contains all the necessary study material for the course. A student logbook provides a permanent record of each flight, indicating the maneuvers and procedures you worked on and how well they were accomplished. There is an outline of what each lesson will entail, a flight manual and work book, block quizzes, a computer and plotter for use on cross-country flights, and the training airplane manual, with operational and maintenance information about the trainer.

This streamlined method of teaching allows the student to work more at his own pace and fit ground-school study into his own schedule rather than having to attend classes. It also eliminates possible confusion and misunderstandings. Students can look at their logbook and be fully aware of what must be achieved before advancing to the next lesson. And, if the instructor can't make a lesson, the student can fly with someone else, who has only to look in the logbook to see exactly where the student stands.

These courses also are integrated with audiovisual

aids as flight preps, "phase checks" where the student demonstrates how well he is going and quizzes that simulate questions on the FAA written exam. After you complete the course, you are well prepared for both the written exam and flight check by the FAA examiner.

This does not mean, however, that smaller independent flying schools without factory affiliation offer second-rate instruction. Quite the contrary. Smaller schools will often provide the kind of relaxed and informal training environment that naturally appeals to many of us. And the sometimes slightly lower cost at these schools is also in their favor. Another advantage is that students often have more of an opportunity to fly a variety of airplanes instead of just the models their school is promoting or selling.

But, assuming a school is FAA approved, whether you choose a large operation or a small independent firm is mostly a matter of personal preference. The best thing to do is check with as many schools as possible in your area. If you know any pilots who earned their tickets at a school you are considering, check with them and see what they recommend.

APPENDIX THREE
Flying Organizations

As in the case of most activities, there are numerous flying clubs and organizations that you can join to pursue your special interests. They range from purely social groups to bodies that lobby in Washington to protect your interests.

Aerobatic Club of America, P.O. Box 11099, Fort Worth, Texas 76110.

Airborne Law Enforcement Association, National Headquarters, c/o Lt. Robert Lund, Kansas Highway Patrol, Topeka, Kansas 66612.

Aircraft Owners and Pilots Association, 4650 East-West Highway, Bethesda, Maryland 20014.

American Aviation Historical Society, Inc., P.O. Box 996, Ojai, California 93023.

American Bonanza Society, Inc., Chemung County Airport, Horseheads, New York 14845.

American Helicopter Society, Inc., 30 East 42nd Street, Suite 1408, New York, New York 10017.

American Navion Society, P.O. Box 1175, Airport Station, Banning, California 92220.

Antique Airplane Association, P.O. Box H, Ottumwa, Iowa 52501.

Association of Aviation Psychologists, 5108 26th Avenue SE, Washington, D.C. 20031.

Cessna 190–195 Owners Association, c/o Thomas Pappas, P.O. Box 952, Sioux Falls, South Dakota 57101.

Civil Air Patrol, Maxwell Air Force Base, Alabama 36112.

Experimental Aircraft Association, Inc., 11311 West Forest Home Avenue, Franklin, Wisconsin 53132.

Flying Architects Association, Inc., c/o Harold J. Westin, 125 Administration Building, Downtown Airport, St. Paul, Minnesota 55107.

Flying Chiropractors Association, c/o Frederic J. Miscoe, D.C., 528 Franklin Street, Johnstown, Pennsylvania 15905.

Flying Dentists Association, c/o Dr. Paul Hoffman, Jr., 10401 Old Georgetown Road, Bethesda, Maryland 20014.

Flying Engineers International, P.O. Box 387, Winnebago, Illinois 61088.

Flying Funeral Directors of America, 678 South Snelling Avenue, St. Paul, Minnesota 55116.

Flying Physicians Association, 801 Green Bay Road, Lake Bluff, Illinois 60044.

Flying Veterinarians Association, c/o Horace G. Blalock, Jr., D.V.M., 2124 Highland Avenue, Augusta, Georgia 30904.

Future Pilots of America, 707 RCA Building, 1725 K Street NW, Washington, D.C. 20006.

Helicopter Association of America, 1156 15th Street NW, Suite 610, Washington, D.C. 20005.

Independent Protective Order of Taildraggers, P.O. Box 2186, Pomona, California 91766.

International Aerobatic Club, P.O. Box 229, Hales Corner, Wisconsin 53130.

International Cessna 170 Association, P.O. Box 3271, Davenport, Iowa 52808.

International Flying Bankers Association, Box 17, Downers Grove, Illinois 60515.

International Flying Farmers, Municipal Airport, Wichita, Kansas 67209.

Lawyer-Pilots Bar Association, P.O. Box 427, Alhambra, California 91802.

Lighter-Than-Air Society, 1800 Triplett Blvd., Akron, Ohio 44306.

National Aero Club, 3861 Research Park Drive, Research Park, Ann Arbor, Michigan 48104.

National Aeronautic Association, Suite 610, Shoreham Building, 806 15th Street NW, Washington, D.C. 20005.

National Association of Flight Instructors, Box N, Washington, D.C. 20014.

National Association of Priest Pilots, 2210 Lincoln Way, Ames, Iowa 50010.

National Aviation Club, 1156 15th Street NW, Washington, D.C. 20005.

National Business Aircraft Association, Inc., Suite 401, Pennsylvania Building, 425 13th Street NW, Washington, D.C. 20004.

National Pilots Association, 806 15th Street NW, Washington, D.C. 20005.

National Real Estate Fliers Association, 402 William Street, Fredericksburg, Virginia 22401.

Negro Airmen International, Inc., P.O. Box 723, Westbury, New York 11590,

Ninety-Nines, Inc., P.O. Box 59964, Will Rogers World Airport, Oklahoma City, Oklahoma 73159.

Organized Flying Adjusters, 1316 Lincoln Rochester Trust Building, Rochester, New York 14604.

OX5 Club of America, 419 Plaza Building, Pittsburgh, Pennsylvania 15219.

Pilots International Association, Inc., 2649 Park Avenue, Minneapolis, Minnesota 55407.

Popular Rotorcraft Association, P.O. Box 2772, Raleigh, North Carolina 27602.

Silver Wings Fraternity, Box 1228, Harrisburg, Pennsylvania 17108.

Soaring Society of America, Inc., Box 66071, Los Angeles, California 90066.

Society of Automotive Engineers, Inc., 2 Pennsylvania Plaza, New York, New York 10001.

United States Parachute Association, P.O. Box 109, Monterey, California 93940.

Wheelchair Pilots Association, c/o Howard Treadwell, 4211 Fourth Avenue South, St. Petersburg, Florida 33711.

Whirley-Girls, Suite 700, 1725 DeSales Street NW, Washington, D.C. 20036.

Wingfoot Lighter-Than-Air Society, 1210 Massillon Road, Akron, Ohio 44315.

Women's National Aeronautical Association of the United States, Inc., Topeka, Kansas 66601.

APPENDIX FOUR
A Glossary of Aviation Terms

AGL
Above ground level.

AIR DENSITY
The mass density of air in terms of weight per unit volume.

AIRFRAME
The fuselage, booms, nacelles, cowlings, fairings, airfoil surfaces—except propellers—and landing gear of a plane, including accessories and controls.

AIRMET
(Contraction for airman's meteorological information). An in-flight weather advisory detailing weather phenomena potentially hazardous to aircraft. An Airmet is of operational interest to all pilots.

AIRPORT ADVISORY SERVICE
A service provided by flight service stations at airports not served by a control tower. Information is provided to landing and departing planes about wind direction and speed, runway in use, altimeter setting, field conditions, whether there is any other traffic in the area, taxi routes and traffic patterns and also instrument-approach procedures.

AIRPORT TRAFFIC AREA
Airspace within a horizontal radius of five statute miles from the center of an airport at which a control tower is operating. It extends from the surface up to, but not including, 3000 feet.

AIRSPEED
A plane's speed through the air, relative to the surrounding air, not to the ground.

AIR TRAFFIC CLEARANCE
An authorization by air traffic control for an airplane to proceed under specified instructions within controlled airspace.

AIR TRAFFIC CONTROL (ATC)
A service to promote safe, orderly and expeditious traffic flow around large airports. ATC is under the jurisdiction of the Federal Aviation Administration.

ALTERNATE (AIRPORT)
An airport at which a plane may land, if the intended airport should become unavailable, i.e., for reasons of unsuitable weather.

ALTIMETER
An aneroid barometer calibrated to show altitude instead of pressure.

ALTITUDE
Height expressed in units of distance above a reference plane, usually above sea level or above the ground.
Correct altitude. Indicated altitude of an airplane altimeter corrected for the temperature of the column of

air below the aircraft. An approximation of true altitude.

Density altitude. The altitude at which air in the standard atmosphere has the same density as air at the point in question. A plane will have the same performance characteristics as it would have in a standard atmosphere at this altitude.

Indicated altitude. Altitude as indicated on a standard airplane altimeter and uncorrected for temperature. When an airplane is on the ground and the altimeter is set to the local station setting, it will read field elevation, or the true altitude of the field.

Pressure altitude. The altitude in the standard atmosphere at which the pressure is the same as at the point in question. Since an altimeter works solely on pressure, this is the uncorrected altitude shown by an altimeter set to standard sea-level pressure (29.92 inches), i.e., when an altimeter is set to 29.92 inches of mercury, indicated altitude and pressure altitude are the same.

Radar altitude. The altitude of an airplane determined by a radar altimeter, which measures the actual distance from the airplane to the ground by means of a downward-directed radar beam.

True altitude. The exact distance of an airplane above mean sea level.

APPROACH CONTROL

A service to control IFR (instrument flight rules) flights arriving or departing or operating near airports, by means of communication between approach controllers and the pilots operating under their supervision. The service is available to VFR traffic on a work-load-permitting basis.

APPROACH SEQUENCE
The order in which aircraft are positioned while waiting approach clearance or while on approach.

AUTOMATIC TERMINAL INFORMATION SERVICE (ATIS)
A continuous broadcast of recorded information over the voice feature of a VOR or ILS at or near the airport in question. The information usually includes details of cloud ceiling, visibility, wind, the current altimeter setting, instrument approach and runways in use.

AVIATION WEATHER OBSERVATION
An evaluation of weather important to aircraft operation. It includes cloud height or vertical visibility, sky cover, horizontal visibility and certain atmospheric phenomena, obstructions to vision, wind speed and direction at the time the observation was made. Complete observations include sea-level pressure, temperature, dew-point temperature, altimeter setting and any pertinent remarks.

BASE LEG
A flight path at approximately a right angle to the landing runway off its approach end and extending from the downwind leg to the intersection of the extended runway center line.

BEARING
In air navigation, the same as azimuth. A bearing is

always *from* a station or other fix, unless specifically stated as *to*.

BRIEFING

Essential information pertaining to a particular flight, i.e., a weather briefing. Briefing also refers to specific instructions to a student pilot prior to a cross-country flight.

CALIBRATED AIRSPEED (CAS)

Indicated airspeed of an airplane, corrected for position and instrument error. Calibrated airspeed is equal to true airspeed in standard atmosphere at sea level.

CATEGORY

(1) With respect to the certification, ratings, privileges and limitations of pilots, it means a broad classification of aircraft. Examples include airplane, rotorcraft, glider and lighter-than-air. (2) With respect to the certification of airplanes, it means a grouping of aircraft upon intended use of operating limitations. Examples include transport, normal, utility, aerobatic, limited, restricted and provisional.

CEILING

The height above the earth's surface of the lowest layer of clouds reported as "broken," "overcast" or "obscuration" and not classified as "thin" or "partial."

CLASS

(1) With respect to the certification, ratings, privileges and limitations of pilots, it means a classification within a category having similar operating characteristics. Examples include single-engine, multiengine, land, water,

gyroplane, helicopter, airship and free balloon. (2) As used with respect to the certification of aircraft, class means a broad grouping of aircraft having similar characteristics of propulsion, flight or landing. Examples include airplane, rotorcraft, glider, balloon, landplane and seaplane.

CLEARANCE
Authorization to follow a specified flight outline. Clearances are issued by a control agency supervising operations in the area in which the flight will take place.

COLD FRONT
Any nonoccluded front, or portion thereof, that moves in such a way that cold air replaces warmer air.

CONTRAIL
A cloudlike streamer frequently observed behind aircraft flying in clear, cold and humid air, caused by the addition to the atmosphere of water vapor from the exhaust.

CONTROL AREA
Airspace of defined dimensions, extending upward from a specified altitude above the surface, within which air-traffic is controlled.

CONTROLLED AIRSPACE
Airspace designated as continental control area, control area, control zone or transition area, within which some or all aircraft may be subject to air traffic control.

CONTROLLER
An air-traffic-control specialist.

CONTROL ZONE
Controlled airspace. A control zone may include one or more airports and is normally a circular area with a radius of five miles, plus any extensions needed to include instrument approach and departure paths.

COORDINATES
Description of a geographical location by latitude and longitude. Latitude is measured north or south from the "zero" line of the equator. Longitude is measured east or west from the "zero" line of the Greenwich meridian.

COURSE
The direction toward the destination as charted, described in degrees of deviation from north. *True course* is measured from true north; *magnetic course* is measured from magnetic north. All courses formed by VORs on sectional charts are magnetic.

CROSS-COUNTRY
A flight between two airports and including a landing at a place more than 25 miles from the point of departure.

CROSSWIND
A wind blowing across the line of flight of an aircraft.

CROSSWIND LEG
A flight path at right angles to the landing runway off its upwind leg.

DEBRIEFING
A discussion of a flight between instructor and student

after the flight is completed, to ensure that the student has understood the particular lesson.

DISTANCE-MEASURING EQUIPMENT (DME)

An electronic interrogation/reply system which provides the pilot with a continuous presentation of distance in nautical miles to the DME site.

DRIFT ANGLE

A horizontal angle between the longitudinal axis of a plane and its path relative to the ground.

DUAL

A flight in which the student flies the aircraft under the supervision of an instructor.

ESTIMATED CEILING

In aviation weather observations, this classification is used when the height of the ceiling layer of clouds or obscuring phenomena aloft has been estimated by the observer.

ETA

Estimated time of arrival.

ETD

Estimated time of departure.

FINAL APPROACH

The flight path of a landing aircraft along the extended runway center line from the base leg to the runway.

FIX

A geographical position determined by visual reference to the surface, by radio navigational aids, celestial plotting or by other navigational means.

FIXED BASE OPERATOR (FBO)
One who provides fuel, oil and usually some maintenance facilities at an airport. Larger FBOs frequently provide an extensive range of ancillary facilities, including food and beverages, flight briefing room, training, sales, service, etc.

FLIGHT PLAN
Specified information about the intended flight of an aircraft, that is filed orally or in writing with an air-traffic-control facility.

FLIGHT SERVICE STATION (FSS)
An FAA-operated, air-ground, voice communications station which relays clearances, requests for clearances and position reports between en-route traffic and the air-route traffic control center. An FSS also provides preflight briefing for both IFR and VFR flights, gives inflight assistance, broadcasts weather information once each hour, monitors radio navigational facilities, accepts VFR flight plans and provides notification of arrival, and also provides notices to airmen about local navigational aids, airfields and other flight data.

FLIGHT TIME
The time from the moment an aircraft first moves under its own power for the purpose of flight until the moment it comes to rest at the next point of landing ("block" or "block-to-block" time).

FLIGHT VISIBILITY
The average forward horizontal distance, from the cockpit of an aircraft in flight, at which prominent unlighted objects may be seen and identified by day and

prominent lighted objects may be seen and identified at night.

HEADING
The direction in which the nose of an airplane points during flight. Corrections made to compensate for wind will cause differences between track and heading. If no correction is made to compensate for wind, differences will occur between track and course as the aircraft drifts.

IFR WEATHER
Route or terminal weather conditions of sufficiently low ceiling and/or visibility to require flight operation under instrument flight rules.

INBOUND
Flying toward a VOR station, toward a fix, toward an L/MF station by ADF or toward an airport on final approach.

INDICATED AIRSPEED
The speed of an aircraft, as shown by its airspeed indicator, and uncorrected for airspeed system errors.

IN-FLIGHT WEATHER ADVISORY
Messages issued to aircraft in flight containing information of potentially hazardous weather conditions.

INSTRUMENT FLIGHT RULES
When weather is below the minimums prescribed for visual flight, pilots must fly in accordance with IFR. Pilots may elect to fly an IFR flight plan during VFR conditions also.

INTERSECTION
A fix established by the intersection of specified radials from VOR stations, or one VOR station and a localizer.

ISOBAR
A line of equal barometric pressure. The pattern of isobars is a key feature of surface-chart interpretation.

ISOGONIC LINES
Lines determined by points at which the amount of magnetic variation is equal.

JET STREAM
A narrow wandering stream of wind with a speed of 50 knots or more, within the normal wind flow at high altitudes.

LOCALIZER
An instrument-landing navigation facility which provides guidance to the runway center line.

MACH NUMBER
The ratio of true airspeed to the speed of sound.

MEAN SEA LEVEL (MSL)
The average height of the surface of the sea for all states of tide; used as a reference for all elevations throughout the United States.

MEASURED CEILING
The ceiling classification applied when cloud ceiling has been determined by: (1) a ceiling light or ceilometer or (2) the known heights of unobscured portions of objects—other than natural landmarks—within one

and a half nautical miles of any runway of an airport. It applies only to clouds and obscuring phenomena aloft and is identified by the ceiling designator "M."

NAVIGATIONAL AID (NAVAID)
A visual or electronic device which provides point-to-point guidance information and/or partial or complete position data to aircraft in flight.

NOTICE TO AIRMEN (NOTAM)
A notice containing essential information about the establishment, condition or change in any part of, or hazard in, the national airspace system.

OCCLUDED FRONT (commonly called *occlusion,* also called a *frontal occlusion*)
A composite of two fronts, as a cold wave overtakes a warm front or quasi-stationary front.

PATWAS (PILOT'S AUTOMATIC TELEPHONE WEATHER ANSWERING SERVICE)
Continuous taped weather information giving the aviation weather forecast with details of the synoptic situation, wind forecasts, weather warnings and, when available, radar reports. In some parts of the country the service is connected to a transcribed weather broadcast (TWEB) system. The service is useful for getting an idea of the "big picture" before calling flight service for a detailed weather briefing.

PILOT IN COMMAND
The pilot responsible for the operation and safety of an aircraft during flight.

PILOT WEATHER REPORT (PIREP)
A report of in-flight weather by an aircraft pilot or crew member.

PITCH
(1) The blade angle of a propeller or (2) the movement of an aircraft about its lateral axis.

POSITION
The geographic location of a plane by visual reference, by means of a radio fix or by any other means; altitude supplements and completes position but is stated separately.

PREVAILING WIND
The wind direction most frequently observed during a given period.

RADIAL
A navigational signal from a VOR or VORTAC, measured as a magnetic bearing from the station.

SEARCH AND RESCUE (SAR)
A service to look for missing aircraft and to help those needing assistance.

SEPARATION
The spacing of aircraft by air traffic control to achieve safe and orderly movement in flight and while landing and taking off.

SIGMET
(Contraction for significant meteorological information.)

A message of particular interest to pilots of *all* aircraft. In the United States, an in-flight weather advisory issued to include tornadoes or squall lines, damaging hail, severe and extreme turbulence, heavy icing and widespread dust storms.

STALL
The flight maneuver or condition in which the air passing over and under the wings stops providing sufficient lift to hold the airplane's altitude. A stall is caused by increasing the angle of attack to a point at which lift degenerates and dies. The cure is to decrease the angle of attack.

TRACK
The flight path made over the ground by an aircraft. A track may also be called a *course* when referring to a charted route and is described in terms of magnetic bearing.

TRAFFIC PATTERN
The traffic flow for aircraft landing at, taxiing on and taking off from an airport. The usual components of a traffic pattern are upwind leg, crosswind leg, downwind leg, base leg and final approach.

TRANSPONDER
A radar receiver-transmitter carried in a plane which selectively responds to ground inquiries. Its reply enables air traffic control to pinpoint an aircraft on the radarscope.

TRUE AIRSPEED
The airspeed of an aircraft relative to undisturbed air.

TURBULENCE
Irregular motion of the atmosphere produced when air flows over a comparatively uneven surface, such as the surface of the earth, or when two air currents flow past or over each other in different directions or at different speeds.

ULTRAHIGH FREQUENCY (UHF)
A frequency band from 300 to 3000 megahertz.

UNICOM
Frequencies authorized for advisory services to private aircraft. Only one such station is authorized at any landing area. The frequency 123.00 MHz is used at airports served by a control tower of FSS and 122.8 used at other landing areas.

VERY HIGH FREQUENCY (VHF)
Frequency band from 30 to 300 megahertz.

VFR CONDITIONS
Basic weather conditions prescribed for flight under visual flight rules.

WARM FRONT
The forward edge of an advancing current of relatively warm air which is displacing a retreating colder mass of air.

Index